Conscious Language™

The Logos of NOW

The Discovery, Code and Upgrade to Our New Conscious Human Operating System.

Robert Tennyson Stevens

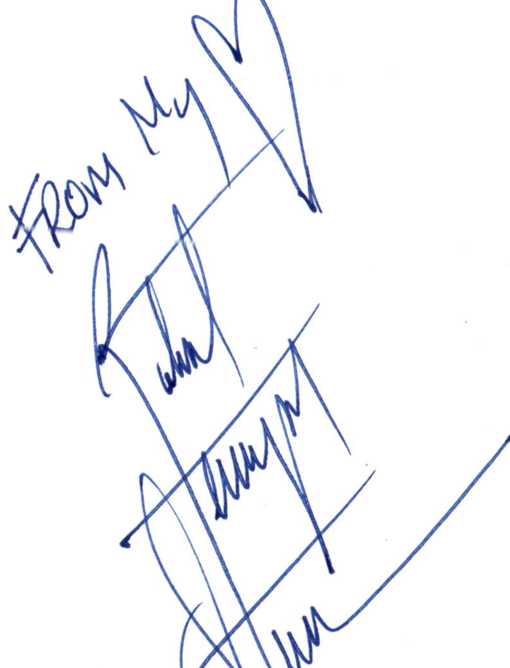

Foreword by *Gregg Braden,* New York Times Best Selling Author

Printed in the United States of America.

Robert Tennyson Stevens
Conscious Language™ , The Logos of NOW
The Discovery, Code and Upgrade to our new Conscious Human Operating System.

ISBN 978-0-9789291-2-1

Co-editors:	Shabari Lynda Bird
	José Ricardo Fuentes
Design:	www.moccadesign.com
Cover Design:	Mignon Zuleika Petrini

Mastery Systems'
Conscious Human Operating System Series

DEDICATION

To my wife, Helena, who has
gone ahead to check out Heaven
and find the place God has prepared for us.

To my Daughters, Mignon and Divinity:
you both are my promise of
Heaven on Earth.

To Humanity
who is remembering Pure Speech,
the Language of our Heart.

Godspeed to us all.

Contents

Section D Appendices

Foreword

How much power do our words really carry? Is it possible that our words—the air that we invite into the deepest recesses of our body and then carefully expel through the sacred organ of our vocal chords—have a power that is so great that it was intentionally confused over 5,000 thousand years ago? What would it mean to re-discover the secret of the language that heals our deepest hurts, breathes life into our greatest joys, and literally creates Reality itself?

The book that you hold in your hand answers these questions and much more! The result of over thirty years of research and the experiences of many thousands of people, *Conscious Language™, The Logos of NOW* is the premier guide to Conscious Language™ in the 21st Century. Through 18 concise chapters, the pioneering work of Robert Tennyson Stevens masterfully leads us on a step by step journey in the new science of *Conscious Language™*; the science of choosing the words that express our true intent, and knowing that our words are the quantum templates of health, abundance, peace and relationships!

Sometimes hilarious and always thought provoking, Robert Stevens has filled *Conscious Language™, The Logos of NOW,* with true life stories and easy to understand examples. Each one invites us to consider how consciously we are using the language of creation in our own lives. By following the exercises, we find that clarity in our words can lead to a clear understanding of life's greatest challenges. Once recognized, we also see how subtle "upgrades" in our language, can change the way we feel about ourselves and what we believe to be true in our world. And why not? After all, the words that we speak are the literal commands to consciousness itself, the quantum "stuff" where everything begins!

Perhaps the 13th Century mystic Rumi best described the power of our relationship to our bodies and our world by saying, "We are the mirror, and the face in the mirror. We are the sweet cold water, and the jar that pours." In other words, through the language of poetry Rumi reminds us of the mystical irony of life. We are creating our reality, as well as experiencing what we have created. We are the artists as well as the art, suggesting that we have the power to alter what we experience.

Today, modern scientists describe precisely the same irony. Using the language of quantum physics rather than poetry, a growing number of leading edge scientists suggest that the universe, and everything in the universe, "is" what it "is" because of consciousness itself—the same consciousness that is affected by our words. In 1967, the pioneering physicist Konrad Zuse married the ideas of a creative consciousness with modern technology and proposed that our universe works like a massive consciousness computer (MIT Technical Translation, 02139, 1970). And just as every computer translates "Input—Commands" into "Output—Results," our cosmic consciousness computer appears to do precisely the same thing!

In this analogy, it is consciousness itself that does the translating. And the reality of our everyday lives is the quantum "Output" of what our deepest beliefs have created. Just as the changes that come from a computer's output must come from within the computer itself, to change the reality of our lives we must change the language that makes our reality as it is. The key is that we must do so while we are still living in the conditions and relationships that formed from our existing use of words and beliefs! This beautiful and powerful fact is where this book comes in. Because we create through the words that carry our deepest beliefs, our language holds the power to tear down or build up, to destroy or create.

But you already know this from personal experience. You know in your own life, for example that you can absolutely devastate a person, shred their confidence, belittle their achievements, and degrade their self worth. You know, as well, that you have the power to elevate another human being to great heights of confidence and joy simply through the words that you share with them. Both can happen without ever touching them physically—we touch one another, and our world, through the power of our words.

Every day we offer the literal input of our word—commands to the consciousness of the universe. Every day consciousness translates our personal and collective code into the reality of our health, the quality of our relationships, and the peace of our world. And this is the great secret of Conscious Language™ that was lost in the land of Babel over 5,000 thousand years ago. The question now is less about whether our words are powerful, and more about how we use the power of language in our lives. Are we willing to honor our gift of language by saying what we really mean, and saying it consciously?

Gregg Braden, New York Times best selling author of:
The Divine Matrix, The God Code, Secrets of the Lost Mode of Prayer, and *The Isaiah Effect*

Logos, noun. (Latin *logos;* Greek *logos,* a word; the word by which the inward thought is expressed, the inward thought itself, from legein, to --speak.)

1. In Greek philosophy, reason, thought of as constituting the controlling principle of the **Universe** and as being manifested my speech.

—Webster's New Twentieth Century Dictionary Unabridged

Universe, noun.

1. Uni, consisting of one only.
2. Verse, a word, poem or song.
3. Universe, one song, one verse, one poem, unified.

Our awareness—that which we are Conscious of being—is the tapestry of our life. Our language is found in every thread and fiber of our reality. By changing one word within ourselves, we expand, contract or alter our Consciousness, our awareness and our reality. The thoughts and conversations of generations before us are still resonating as true and real in our lives. Many of these language patterns and beliefs are less than our highest truths. There are greater truths, and more wonderful realities awaiting us all. Our language will expand with our Consciousness. Our Consciousness will expand with our language. Our Words hold the key to our new Heaven on Earth. May each Word we speak be our Conscious Prayer coming into reality now and now and now. Life is urging us all to awaken! "Awakening to what?" you may ask. Listen to your Heart. Find the Language of your own Heart. This book is a tool to access your Heartdrive with new Heartware.

In the beginning
was the Word...

By the word of the LORD were the heavens made; and all the host of them by the breath of his mouth. For he spake, and it was done; he commanded, and it stood fast. Psalms 33:6, 9

PREFACE

Reading this book offers a new possibility, a new exactness to the personal *respons-ability* of you, the reader and I, the author, to awaken to exactly how life situations have transpired in our life and what to do, through Language awareness, to change our life situations, into our full manifest potential. Within the body of this book I will demonstrate some of my own self-coaching upgrades including "cancel clear" and "in the past."

> "Language is the blood of the soul into which thoughts run and out of which they grow."
> Oliver Wendell Homes

We have arrived to where we are through our current Language and Consciousness.

Congratulate yourself. You may discover, as I have, we have done amazingly well by using a Language System full of viruses and glitches. You may also discover how to upgrade every aspect of your life, from inside out. The material in this book is dangerous to exposed and hidden limiting beliefs. Please use this material to empower yourself, more wonderfully than you already are and to fulfill your Dreams. Changing a way of thinking, speaking and listening can take a life time or a nano second. For the dedicated seeker of truth, start by choosing to "make it easy" i.e. "I choose to make my personal life upgrades fun and easy."

Words are how we communicate, think and even feel. Language is as integral to our species as an operating system is to a computer. The glitches in our thinking and speaking crash our dreams as quickly as a pesky virus can mess up our computer. Words "rule" because they shape Consciousness. For a few thousand years, humanity has been using a fairly old system of communication. In this system, the belief in "I want,", "I can't," "It's hard," vagueness and impersonal communications were normal. "Lack" happened seemingly out of the blue. Dis-ease was a force beyond the control of most humanity. Success had laws, used by the successful—sometimes with understanding—and misunderstood by the unsuccessful. Maybe it was genetic? Maybe it was fate. Maybe it was beyond our scope of power to understand as human beings. Or is it?

> "Every individual is at once the beneficiary and the victim of the linguistic tradition into which he has been born — the beneficiary inasmuch as language gives access to the accumulated records of other people's experience, the victim in so far as it confirms him in the belief that reduced awareness is the only awareness and as it bedevils his sense of reality, so that he is all too apt to take his concepts for data, his words for actual things."
>
> Aldous Huxley

In this treatise, we will explore the huge possibility we have simply spoken into, thought into, or accepted our reality, in words, *before* or as it became reality. Our Consciousness is the doorway to our experience and reality. We are the ones to confirm and consent to our situations in life by our thoughts, feelings, and especially our words as scientifically and mechanically as any other law of the Universe. By taking ownership of our conditions in our lives and becoming aware of our Language shaped thoughts we can powerfully change our life situations. Our everyday language reveals exactly what we are agreeing with and therefore creating. By a simple shift in our language we can shift our Consciousness and experience our Dreams as reality.

> "Language is the roadmap of a culture. It tells you where its people came from and where they are going. "
>
> Rita Mae Brown

We do have a choice. Remember choice? What is your choice? By making a new Conscious Choice we can begin the Upgrade of Conscious Language™ and when you are ready, take the next step to the language and experience of "Mastery."

"Ask and it shall be given you; seek and ye shall find; knock and it shall be opened unto you:" Matthew 7:7

GENTLY APPROACHING SCRIPTURE

Scriptures have been used down through the ages to Bless or bind, help or hinder, forgive or judge, separate or unify. Like any form of power, humanity has used scriptures to blame and bless. I have allowed myself to let Scripture touch my Heart with the Spirit of Truth. I invite each of you journeying through these pages, whatever your Spiritual inclination may be, to ask God, your God, The One in Your Heart, to awaken any and all Truth found in or through the words and ideas presented here. May you be more fully One with your Creator, as you read each page and by the power of your own choice, prayer, decree, focus and intention.

A Decree is a Law: Something spoken with authority and conviction.

"In all your getting, get understanding." Proverbs 4:7

I have presented this material to Fortune 500 companies, governmental agencies, business executives, sales people, parents, children, teachers, ministers, rabbis, gurus, saints, and sinners alike. Language is universal and a special creative quality bestowed upon us by the Author of Humanity and the Universe. In my seminars and talks, one of my first tasks is to help us all find common ground about the God thing. More people have been killed in the name of some God than I care to imagine. Whatever name I use for God—Creator, Buddha, Christ, Allah, Jehovah, I AM that I AM—if it does not ring your bell, please translate my words into your words of Truth. The message in this book is designed to reach your Heart, whatever your spiritual inclination may be and is exceedingly timely for Humanity. Finding where we can communicate is one of the Mission's within this book. Thank you ahead of time for adjusting your inner ears to listen with your inner Heart through what ever words I use. Communication starts with intention to commune—to be at one.

> *"For there are three that bear record in heaven, the Father, the Word and the Holy Ghost: and these three are one."*
> *1 John 5:7*

AUTHOR'S NOTES

> "Limited beliefs are committed to their own survival even unto the demise of the physical vehicle in which they reside until they meet a commitment to change the limitation into some powerful and specific Blessing."
>
> Helena T. Stevens

The information in this book is taken from my experiences with thousands of people who have made a commitment to be a "committed listening" and to play 125%. Give yourself permission to test every concept, definition, suggestion and idea for accuracy and truth. I have learned a great lesson over the years: My limiting beliefs are committed to being what they are—limited.

To change limited beliefs, commit to upgrade into Victorious beliefs, fully.

Capitalizations are used to Develop Full Meanings throughout this book (Just so those who have editorial skills know we know).

IMAGINATION ACTIVATION

THE POWER OF IMAGINATION

Over the years sharing powerful paradigm shifting options with individuals, organizations, corporations, families, and couples, I have learned the importance of letting the subconscious mind or feeling nature know ahead of time "where it is going" and "how it is going to get there." Before beginning this journey of language, I recommend gifting your own Inner Being with the following exercise.

The following exercise is best done before reading this book and again at any time limiting beliefs appear to struggle with your upgrades.This powerful exercise creates new synaptic linkages, resulting in higher choices residing in our mind and emotions. The practice of imagining what our life is like now, as if our life was lived using conscious creative thoughts and language, results in a life lived from our Heart's highest choices. When we know where we are going, the trip is much smoother and the desired outcomes manifest with greater EASE.

> *"Declaring the end from the beginning, and from ancient times the things that are not yet done, saying, My counsel shall stand, and I will do all my pleasure." Isaiah 46:10*

Imagination Activation Exercise

Imagine you have experienced open, honest, direct, heartfelt, outcome-oriented communication and have used Conscious Creative Language all your life.

Imagine you were conceived consciously by your Mother and Father, who planned for you, chose you, prepared for you with their own personal, deep, sacred focus and commitment.

Imagine you were received at your birth by the hands of many loving attendants and family members who received you as the Divinity you are.

Imagine you remember who you really are. Fully place yourself in this newly imagined state of awareness.

Coming from your newly imagined state of awareness (make it the facts of your New current existence), describe what your life is now like.

Ask yourself:

- What am I doing?
- Who is with me?
- What is around me?
- What is home like?
- What is my workplace like?
- What are my relationships like?
- What does my life look like?
- Smell like?
- Feel like?
- Sound like?

Imagine a Genie is instantly giving you your every wish. As you write this on a separate sheet of paper or even begin a new journal:

- Be sure to be vivid and specific.
- Write your responses personally, in first person, with feeling.
- Be free from your editor mind and write what comes to you as it comes to you.
- Be spontaneous and feel each word as you write it down.

SECTION A

WHAT IS CONSCIOUS LANGUAGE™?

CHAPTER 1

LANGUAGE AND CONSCIOUSNESS

Language, speech, words, and ultimately thoughts are the casting of spells. Our language shapes energy into matter. When we learn how to "spell" a word, we learn how to shape the sounds or letters of a word with meaning and feeling. If what we say matters to us, it ultimately influences "matter" or turns into matter—physical manifestation.

As you will discover, our language is the shaper of our world, the "spell" of our reality. Health, disease (dis-ease), happiness, sadness, abundance, poverty, survival and "thrival" are all Decreed by the individual or group into reality through our Consciousness. Our language shapes our Consciousness. As you will further understand through the Domains of Language, Scriptures and Gospels (God-Spells) our words are of the same creative force and powerful activity as God's Word. All Creation is God's. We are God's energy. We use God's Energy all day long to create Heaven or hell. We have been somewhat handicapped until now. We were given a confused language. I call it the "Babel Virus." It is essential we—humanity—know what the "Babel Virus" is and what influence it is having on our Consciousness through our inner and outer speech.

> "Human beings do not live in the objective world alone, nor alone in the world of social activity as ordinarily understood, but are very much at the mercy of the particular language which has become the medium of expression for their society. It is quite an illusion to imagine that one adjusts to reality essentially without the use of language and that language is merely an incidental means of solving specific problems of communication or reflection. The fact of the matter is that the 'real world' is to a large extent unconsciously built up on the language habits of the group ... We see and hear and otherwise experience very largely as we do because the language habits of our community predispose certain choices of interpretation."
>
> Edward Sapir

[1]And the whole earth was of one language and of one speech.
[4]And they said, Go to, let us build us a city and a tower,
whose top may reach unto heaven; and let us make us a
name, lest we be scattered abroad upon the face of the whole
earth. [5]And the LORD came down to see the city and the
tower, which the children of men builthed. [6]And the LORD
said, Behold, the people is one and they have all one lan-
guage; and this they begin to do: and now nothing will be
restrained from them, which they have imagined to do. [7]Go
to, let us go down and there confound their language, that
they may not understand one another's speech. [8]So the
LORD scattered them abroad from thence upon the face of
all the earth: and they left off to build the city. [9]Therefore is

the name of it called Babel; because the LORD did there confound the language of all the earth: and from thence did the LORD scatter them abroad upon the face of all the earth.
Genesis 11:1, 4—9

For those who have a Scriptural focus, this quote speaks for itself. For those who have a different focus, I share a quote one of my mentors shared with me many years ago:

"Contempt, prior to complete investigation will enslave a person to ignorance."
Dr. John W. Ray

I did not start with a scriptural background. I have found Scripture by "accident." If the Bible is a book of Truth which I have experienced it is—thousands of times—and if the Tower of Babel event is true and happened; then the Consciousness which inspired these Scriptures must have had a reason for confusing the language of the people at that time.

The way I see it, if a child got hold of a gun and was playing with it, good parents would take it away for safety. The same thing may be true with our Divine Parent, realizing humanity of that period was using the all powerful tongue to create an external monument to an internal and eternal Heaven.

Neither shall they say, Lo here! or, lo there! for, behold, the kingdom of God is within you.
Luke 17:21

"If your language is confused, your intellect, if not your whole character, will almost certainly correspond."
Sir Arthur Quiller Couch

By confusing our language, we may have been spared total destruction from the mis-use of the power of Language. This confused language saved humanity's life, yet it is still operating today. I believe now is the time to awaken from the "Curse of Babel," know the Kingdom of God is within and realize the Divine Temple within each of us. I believe the time has arrived to remember Pure Speech, Conscious Language™, the

Language of our Heart, The Language of Now, the Language of I AM That I AM. Please join me and thousands of other Consciousness students in remembering Pure Speech. May we use our Words to heal, to bless, to prosper and to thrive from this moment forward.

Awakening from the "Curse of Babel" requires determination, Love, Faith and commitment to self correct our Consciousness and life actions. It will also take Grace, lots of Grace.

> **"For then will I turn to the people a pure language—also translated: pure speech—that they may all call upon the name of the LORD, to serve him with one consent." Zephaniah 3:9**

Many simple and very powerful statements of Truth have been shown to me by Grace at an early age. I have found Truth only becomes Truer. The passage, *"Decree a thing and it shall be established unto you"* is very real and at the heart of my sharing. An important key is to understand what a Decree actually is. Finding out what a Conscious, Life Giving Decree is and what an unconscious decree is becomes vital to the person who is committed to thriving and living their Glorious, Successful, Happy and Abundant Life.

> "The quality of our thoughts is bordered on all sides by our facility with language."
> J. Michael Straczynski

By realizing (real-eyes-ing) what we are actually saying to ourselves with our inner speech and to others with our spoken word, awakens our "New Self" within us. This "New Self" is already here. Our "New Self" functions in truth. Our "New Self" operates Consciously. I define the operations of this "New Self" awareness as our "Conscious Human Operating System" (C-HOS). By determining to speak (inner speech and outer speech) only what we choose to have come into manifestation now and continuously brings forth quantum levels of ever expanding success.

The systematic language code provided in this book acts as a guide, memory agent or stimulator for upgrading our lives, communications, prayers, creativity and relationships. Your commitment to your Heart's Pure Speech will be what resurrects your own world into your Heart's manifest desire. Ultimately the process of remembering the consciousness of our Creator will awaken our "I AM That I AM." This is both practical and Spirit filled.

SPEECH

> "Death and Life are in the power of the tongue."
>
> Proverbs 18:21

Speech is the conscious direction of breath from our lungs turned into sound currents crossing over our vocal cords. Those sound currents, shaped by our tongue, mouth, and lips, become words which have power to give life or take life.

All language is vibration. Vibration includes sound and light. Language is the process of Spirit (breath, inspiration) becoming reality.

"And the Word became flesh." John 1:14

By bringing our awareness to our Language we expand our awareness—a good thing. By becoming Conscious of speaking, thinking and hearing limiting language we are able to make changes in our words, thoughts, and feelings and speak, think and hear new positive, helpful, supportive, specifically healing words. We can begin to rewrite our scripts (scripture) in love, abundance, joy, unity, Grace, and ease. Conscious Language™ is the remedy for the Babel Virus because it causes us to be Conscious of our expression and creation.

Some students of Life will start by changing their state of "wanting" (lacking) , to "choosing" and on to "having." Some will start by moving from being disconnected (the money, that family, their world) into being connected (my money, my family, our world). Hundreds of simple language and consciousness shifts are presented in this book. As simple as each of these expression upgrades appear, I invite you to prepare yourself:

> "Language shapes the way we think and determines what we can think about."
> Benjamin Lee Whorf

Language changes are extremely powerful!

Small upgrades in our lives are subtle. Going to a slightly newer version of some software program or buying a new automobile of the same style one year newer is not very noticeable. Upgrading to Conscious Language™ is more like going from the much older computer operating system DOS to the new and very robust operating system Microsoft's Windows XP Pro. Imagine the consciousness of the authors of DOS compared to the authors of XP Pro—even if they were some of the same people. Many of our computer programs and computer accessories will not even run on such a large upgrade.

Our limited belief systems, encoded to maintain us being confused, blocked and stifled, will also have major changes to go through in the upgrade to Conscious Language™. A computer is not a feeling, emotional, living, breathing, inspired human being. You are! Humanity's upgrade process is exponentially more challenging. Our thoughts, feelings, memories, both genetic and experiential, are stored on in our bodies and on our "Heart Drive."

> "What is now proved was once only imagined."
> William Blake

Upgrading to a new Conscious Human Operating Systems will take new "Heartware."

Lucky for us, the Heartware required is already installed on our Heart Drive by our Maker.

The following upgrade is best approached carefully, honestly, prayerfully and lovingly. "I choose to make this fun and easy" is a great affirmation for what you are about to initiate or enhance in your life.

> **May you instantly and in Perfect Divine Order connect with the Truth within your Heart of Hearts and confidently speak only what you choose to have manifest now and continuously with ease and Grace. And so it is… And it is good, very good.**

CHAPTER 2

REMEMBERING CONSCIOUS LANGUAGE™

My passion for language started in 1968. A university professor, Bryce Zender, at Western Michigan University noticed I looked different than the rest of the Marketing and Business School students (I had long hair, it was the 60's). Bryce was very committed to helping students find their life mission and he invited me to do an independent study of my choice. I selected the Hopi Indians as my topic, figuring I already knew enough about them, their prophecy, life style, culture, and beliefs from my Native American study. Bryce suggested I study the Hopi Language, of which I knew nada, zip, nothing. With some coaxing I agreed.

Little did I know what was about to happen to my Consciousness. I was handed a book titled, *Language, Thought and Reality*, by Benjamin Lee Whorf. This little brown paperback book could have been named the red pill after Neo's experience in the Consciousness blockbuster movie, *The Matrix* because my known "world" was about to become "whirled" in a very new direction.

Whorf was an engineer by trade and fascinated with the structure of Language as it shapes a culture's concept of reality. He approached language the way a quantum physicist approaches energy waves. Studying Whorf's research on the Hopi Language expanded my consciousness in a dynamic new way for my 19 years on Planet Earth.

I found myself reading a passage over and over as my consciousness shifted. The idea: our language shapes our reality; that each language defines an entirely different reality through different words (linguistic determination); that space and time were different for the Hopi. The idea that the Hopi had no "space" or "time" in their language in the way I had space and time challenged the very core of the "reality" I was living in.

> "After long and careful study and analysis, the Hopi language is seen to contain no words, grammatical forms, constructions or expressions that refer directly to what we call "time." or to past, present or future or to enduring or lasting or to motion as kinematics rather than dynamic (i.e. as a continuous translation in space and time rather than as an exhibition of dynamic effort in a certain process) or that even refer to space in such a way as to exclude that element of extension or existence that we call "time," and so by implication leave a residue that could be referred to as "time." Hence, the Hopi language contains no reference to "time," either explicit or implicit."
>
> Benjamin Lee Whorf

I was being stretched in every direction and my known "box" of my current reality was dissolving (morphing) quickly.

Whorf's work was like a parakeet giving birth to an ostrich for my Consciousness. It took almost a year to write my thesis. I was so "expanded" or should I say "dumbfounded" (I found my dumb self, in the past, cancel clear[1]), I finally just gave quotes from my research for my thesis, instead of giving my own opinions. I realize my birthing process continued on for decades. My

[1] "In the past, cancel clear" is a declaration I utter every time I choose to neutralize the power of an statement and cancel its creative energy. See "Decree a thing" page 160

hoped-for A turned into the lowest grade Bryce had ever given, a B-, as his form of retribution for not offering my own ideas on this language thing. Bryce, if you are still here, please know it has taken me 37 years to finish my thesis which you are now reading. I thank you, from my Heart, for your guidance.

WHAT WAS SO STRETCHING?

Things like understanding the **Hopi did not have a word for *now* because they couldn't get out of now to have to use the word now to get back to now.** What? And they were so here they experienced being one with the rock, not the rock was over there, no, the rock is one with them right here. Huh? Only they would not even say it that way (you know, English vs. Hopi, apples vs. tractors). I studied words and conjugation of verbs to begin to understand these Blessed People's awareness which was so very different from the language (operating) system I was using.

> **"We cut nature up, organize it into concepts and ascribe significances as we do largely because we are parties to an agreement to organize it in this way—an agreement that holds throughout our speech community and is codified in the patterns of our language. The agreement is, of course, an implicit and unstated one, but its terms are absolutely obligatory; we cannot talk at all except by subscribing to the organization and classification of data which the agreement decrees." Whorf—1956.**

To confound matters even more, I had just read Baba Ram Das' book *Be Here Now* and was greatly wowed by this cosmic explorer turned Holy Man and his ah-ha of studying with all these Eastern Masters and boiling down his experience of these "advanced souls" to the experience of "Be here now!"

Then I study Whorf, who finds this Tribe who have a language shaping a reality where they are so here and now they do not even have the words, here and now. Go figure…

> "Our minds are often permeated by memories of the past or worries about the future. What gets missed is the present and right there in the moment is the doorway into timelessness."
> Ram Das

"A change in language can transform our appreciation of the Cosmos[2]." Benjamin Lee Whorf

Then was 1968. Yes, I still ascribe to some forms of time. Through thousands of interactions, coaching, trainings and teachers, I have woken up to the creative "Code" of language. What I call Conscious Language™. My focus in this writing is to share with you a simple and systematic way of creating New Realities according to the Spirit within our Heart.

I invite you to discover a Consciousness stretch as vast as my own has been, is, and will continue to be, by waking up to Conscious Language™.

For over 35 years of playing and sharing with many enlightened beings, I have discovered some very helpful suggestions and experiences to pass on to you and your loved ones. Your ease and comfort in Decreeing your New Life (Inner Life, Successful Life, Spirit Filled Life) happens when you revise your current reality into your heart's desire. We still have our "mountain" to move. Instead of using a toothpick you have the opportunity to use the *"Mondo—Mega—Dozer"* of Conscious Language™.

"So shall my word be that goeth forth out of my mouth: it shall not return unto me void, but it shall accomplish that which I please and it shall prosper in the thing whereto I sent it." Isaiah 55:11

---

[2] Benjamin Lee Whorf, -1956? Language, Thought & Reality. MIT Press: Cambridge p. 262-3

UPGRADING MY LIFE THROUGH CONSCIOUS LANGUAGE™

I proceeded to integrate the language mystery with the varied studies of my life path, including: alternative health, Consciousness, meditation, prayer, herbology, alternative energy, solar energy, green building, decreeing, parenting, success, sales, Spirit—God in every form and path I could find—relationships, business, and music. Each topic or area of enthusiastic interest seemed a study in itself until one day the whole puzzle came together within me, like spokes of a wheel, in one central hub, one place in my Heart with language at the core.

> "The individual's whole experience is built upon the plan of his language. "
>
> Henri Delacroix

One momentous day I realized my language, my own words, thoughts, feelings and all my expressions, were shaping my own reality, moment by moment by moment, word by word by word. I found my own thoughts (inner speech) was pre-describing (pre-tending, pre-ordering) my outer reality. I began to hear those I personally lived and worked with and professionally coached and trained directly Decreeing, through their words, their positive or negative "reality." I found the core cause. I found the code of reality.

I found each of our realities was being shaped directly by our inner speech and outer Languaging, consciously or unconsciously, exactly as we were saying it.

I began to hear creation at the level of First Cause. I found the Universe and our subconscious were and are connected and *literal.*

Our language is self fulfilling prophecy.

> "Whatever we think in words comes forth to the degree we feel it and to our degree of specificity".
>
> Author

Before my current approach to Conscious Language™, those who knew me in my early 20's most likely would say that I was already passionate about the role of language in my life. My veilrending awakening I was about to go through came as a huge surprise to me, very unexpectedly, like a thief in the night.

Then an experience happened with a very good friend of mine who was involved in taking classes with me and doing Body Electronics—a form of sustained acupressure developed by one of my mentors, Dr. John W. Ray, ND. My friend was a tool and dye man near Ann Arbor, Michigan. Alternative health was a brand new field for him. After observing miraculous healing of broken bones and other miracles through Body Electronics, he had committed to be a trainer of B.E. Broken bones heal very quickly in this system. My friend began to wonder (worry?) if he would be able to heal something like a broken bone. The Universe gave him his answer. To make a very long story short, four days from his questioning his ability, he was with his estranged, soon to be divorced wife, and their children at a park. He was in tremendous pain about the upcoming divorce not being of his own choice. As he began to leave the park he said to himself, "I just don't understand, I don't understand why my wife is leaving me." He spoke these words with very deep feeling and with repetition. As he stepped off the curb he twisted and fractured his left leg.

You will understand through these pages how our every word is heard and is made manifest by our Creator within us.

Did he create the broken leg?

What I discovered in that moment changed my entire understanding of Language and its role in reality. In the Body

Electronics (B.E.) process, the individual remembers and relives the trauma just like it happens. Until the B.E. session, he had no Conscious knowledge of what he was thinking or saying before or at the time of the injury. He just knew he broke his leg. "Pain is the capstone to memory," Dr. John Ray would tell us. By loving the pain, the memory comes back, and if we re-live and love the experience with all the corresponding thoughts, words and emotions, the body will heal, in reverse order as the symptoms have appeared. During my friend's B.E. session he remembered feeling and saying, "I don't understand, I just don't understand why we can't be together." I was present at his session and heard him re-live his experience while his bone was mending (yes it healed right then) and I "heard" his words on a whole new level.

Words spoken with specificity and feeling equals manifestation.

I now know what he was creating with his words. "I" is the creative mind, the "I AM that I AM." "I don't understand" means "I don't stand under" myself. The more specific we are, the more feelings we express, the quicker the manifestation. Simultaneously as he steps off the curb, he is saying "I don't understand" and twists and breaks his leg. Did he create it? Yes! Exactly and literally as he said it. His subconscious mind responded to the words, literally and made it so he could "not stand under" himself, thus a broken leg.

> *"By your words you shall be justified and by your words you shall be condemned." Matthew 12:37*

This experience, this simple Body Electronics session, with 50 to 60 people in the class, rocked my world. At that moment I understood, for the first time, how language works. I was shocked awake. I continue to experience Language on entirely new and revealing levels.

THE SUBCONSCIOUS MIND IS LITERAL

When my friend said, "I don't understand" with all his feeling and in repetition, his subconscious mind heard him LITERALLY and brought about his words exactly as he used them. "I don't understand" being also translated "I don't stand under myself." At that moment, there were about 10 more sessions going on, with other experiences being relived. Not similar in broken bones, yet similar in language statements which were brought about exactly as the person stated them. My eyes and ears were opened in a new way. I began to hear the code of Consciousness, the script of creation, the obedience of creation to our every word. I began to hear and experience the Prophetic Nature of Language. In this moment I knew: changing our Consciousness with our tongue precedes any physical modality or remedial agent. In the beginning of all created situations is the Word!

> *"For as a man thinketh in his heart, so is he."*
> *Proverbs 23:7*

My new awareness: when we change a belief system in thought, word and emotional pattern, we change our body, we change our situation and we change our reality.

When we say specifically what we choose with aligned feelings our subconscious, being literal, brings our choice into being.

> **The more specific we are, the more instantaneous the manifestation. The more we feel, the more powerful the manifestation.**

How many times have you heard or said things like, "It kills me," or "I don't get it," or "I will never understand?"

> **Like any operating system, the nature and the dynamic of the system is the boundary of the system. Our Language sets the capability, the boundary and the function of our system which becomes our Reality.**

With an operating system of "want, can't, struggle, fear, and worry" our boundaries are by definition, limiting. The Babel Virus is built on confusion. We may have been conceived in the Babel Virus. We may actually be thinking in the Babel Operating System right this second. Waking up to Clarity and Unity is our job now.

Anything less than the Spirit of I AM That I AM contains Babel.

RESEARCH AND DEVELOPMENT

I tested my newly gained awareness in my alternative health career. People would come in to receive some support on some "problem." I would ask them the question "Why are you here?" Their answer would reveal how we as humans decree our reality one word at a time. Every state or condition experienced by anyone is believed in, is described with exacting detail and is agreed with; through thought, shaped by spoken or inner language into symptoms (anything less than optimal health) and life conditions.

I commonly heard things like:

Statement ➡	**Consequence**
"I can't stand my roommate."	Their symptoms would be some challenge standing up.
"I hate my mother's anger."	Their symptoms would be some thyroid or energy challenge.
"I don't see how I can forgive them."	Their symptoms would be some vision or eye challenge.
"It is so hard to handle the stress."	Their symptoms would be some muscular hand challenge.[3]

[3] More information is available in the *Sacred Body Language Translations* DVDs,. CDs,and book. Information included in appendices.

These phrases would give the ever active and obedient unconscious mind definite direction in some limited way, which would show up as a health challenge.

Limiting language shapes reality by shaping our Consciousness.

Whatever the modality of healing, type of coaching, situation in life, I found—and still find—Language Upgrades to be essential. They adjust the first cause which quickly adjusts the secondary symptoms. In other words, Changing Language as the primary healing strategy gives the most effective results.

You will discover our language is self-fulfilling prophecy and is simple to change. The key is knowing what to change our current state into…

THE ROLE OF SPECIFICITY

When guiding my class participants, health clients, and myself to transform the limiting statements of what was "not going well," I asked, "What is (your) my goal for my (your) health?" they usually gave some very vague and disconnected idea of improving "this" or "that" or "not having this pain" or "that stress." Each statement was frequently so incomplete and undirected, the path of the subconscious, Super-Conscious, or for that matter my own consciousness was at a loss to help them attain anything.

Examples: What is your goal?

"I want to get better."	*Want* is lack, *better* is vague.
"To improve and not be sick all the time."	*improve* is vague, *not be* is death—*sick all the time* is what they did not choose or the anti-goal.
"To stop being so co-dependent."	*stop being* is death, so co-dependent is vague and does not define what they choose to change into.
"To have perfect health."	vague, what is perfect to you?
"I would like to improve my digestion."	*Would like* to refers to some future time. Like is indirect.

I compare our vague Babel to going to a restaurant with the wait person coming over and asking you, "What do you want?" and you say, "food." Not quite enough information for the server to bring you a satisfying meal.

Babel has been in operation for a long time and has, until now, become our automatic unconscious operating system.

Another example:

"Honey, will you marry me?" "I would like to."	Indirect and weak. Frequently the response was just an "I don't know" or "you know" or "if I could, I would like to," "if I can…"

Awakening to Conscious Language™ is really awakening to the system of the Divine way of life. Once we get it, it is easy. For now, just be alert to the idea and importance of specificity. I practice seeing in pictures what I have just communicated and what others are communicating. If I like the picture I see, the communication is usually clear and definite. If the communication is vague, only a vague sort of hazy picture will emerge. If it is limiting, I replace the picture immediately and suggest a new phrase to the speaker.

Specificity brings up feelings.

Feeling is essential for our Words to manifest. Hidden and suppressed feelings are very comfortable with vagueness and disconnectedness. Vagueness keeps our limitations in status quo.

Honey, can we improve our relationship? Sure honey. Sure because there is no real action plan, no commitment to voice, no job descriptions to accept or delegate, only a vague idea of something, some day, some where, improving. "Sure honey," commonly followed next by, "No problem."

The role of language is the agreement we make with our situations.

The study of the Hopi Language via Whorf and my own research opened my eyes to the role language plays in shaping reality of any culture. My Language shapes my culture. Microsoft's Language shapes their culture. IBM's Language shapes their culture. Shell Oil's Language shapes their culture. This truth goes for our health communities, business communities, governing communities, spiritual communities, international communities, family communities, and so on.

I found my study was not just about a tribe who had a different reality. This was about my tribe, my family, my culture. It seemed a lot of folks did not have a clue what they were saying, let alone know the results of what they were speaking into their lives. I was on to something big. I still Am.

The awakening of our full creative potential requires each of us being fully present within ourselves and partnering with each other.

I partner with you through the rest of these pages and beyond. We are all benefited by partnership.

Is it time for you to be fully awake? I say, "Yes!" What do you say?

When I speak first person, personal and specific about my goal, or support someone else to do the same, manifestation happens quickly. This is very important!

JUST THE BEGINNING...

In my on going awakening process and my discovery of the power of Language, I began to add Conscious Language™ to my classes and talks. My former modus operandi was to share what was working in my life and inspire others to learn it too (OK, more like enthusiastically drag people into their outcomes, in the past, I affirm[4]). Many of my close friends then, and I AM very sure, now, will attest to the former "dragging" process. (Oops! Forgive me Loved Ones for my compulsions of the past).

I remember coming home late one Sunday night from a workshop I was attending and shopping at a 24-hour grocery store in Kalamazoo, Michigan. I turned the corner of one of the isles and saw some very good friends at the far end of the isle. I waved and I continued to shop, heading in their direction. I found their deserted cart around the corner of the aisle, loaded with their weekly groceries. My friends were nowhere in sight. Later they told me they knew I had just returned home from a class and probably had some new healing program I was going to make them do. They bolted. I recommend you find another way than demanding everyone be healthy and Conscious. Since we all use language and we talk out loud, the propensity to coach everyone is pretty inviting. I suggest finding another path. Being an example works better and allows people to stay in the store with you.

"Wherefore by their fruits ye shall know them." Matthew 7:20

---

[4] "In the past, I affirm" See note page 22.

THE LANGUAGE CODE IN SCRIPTURE

I have a very good friend who knows more about more things than anyone I have met. At one point during a meal following my very consistent language "coaching" my friend announced he was finally fed up with my "language suggestions" and let me know in no uncertain terms the language thing was "off course" for him, "only semantics," and "no big deal." In other words, lay off, Stevens, you are bugging me big time!

A week later, my friend's complaint about the language thing being "off course" was going through my head while I planned my next 3 month schedule of classes. Being co-dependent and needing approval back then I sat at my desk while doing my planning, pushing the reminder note to schedule the "Power of the Spoken Word" class further and further away.

My little self was saying how much more accepted and easily approved of I felt when I did the health and herb classes and how uncomfortable it was—I was—with sharing the language thing (approval factor in the negative). The reminder note was making its way to the edge of the back of my desk ready to fall to the floor when my Inner Spirit got my attention. A battle ensued between my co-dependent self and my Great Self. I got hot and itchy and started to squirm. I finally said to myself "Man, what's up?" I knew I needed assistance from on High.

Trusting God would answer my every question I needed to know right now about this "Power of the Spoken Word" class, I stood up and closed my eyes. I was at my health desk, where my extensive health library was and reached up on the top shelf, not having a clue what was on that shelf. With the question in my Heart, I asked, "God, Power of the Spoken Word Class, Yes or No?" I grabbed a book (A Scofield Bible it turned out, the only one in this library), my eyes still closed, pulled it down to my desktop, opened the book, eyes still closed, put my finger somewhere on a page I had opened and opened my eyes. Here is what I saw:

> *"Thou shalt also decree a thing and it shall be established unto thee: and the light shall shine upon thy ways."* Job 22:28

I was brought to full attention. My ducky bumps were having ducky bumps. I had chills running up and down my spine and remembering to breathe was a challenge. My Heart and eyes flowed with tears of great gratitude. When God answers we surely know it. I allowed myself to integrate and breathe and actually stood up and saluted my Lord, my "I AM," my God and said, "Yes God! I have my marching papers."

"Decree a thing and it shall be established unto you" is the first of many instructions I received from the "ask, point and read" system of research. I will share, from my Heart, instructions and Scriptural quotes revealed to me, as they are very personal Gifts from my Creator. I simply and humbly share my experience. I trust you will listen to your own Sacred Heart.

We all deserve to know the Truth, to have our tongue and mind and Heart connected with our Spirit.

> **I believe the way we Glorify our Creator is by living abundantly, in joy and health with our Beloveds.**

Let us all remember, we have a choice on how we live our lives. *"Choose ye this day whom ye shall serve."*

There is more to the story. Much more! If you are wondering if this is a religious story, I prefer to say this is a rich Spiritual, Spirit filled story. Every person who has diligently applied the techniques in this book has experienced a major upgrade of their Spiritual, physical, financial, and social lives. I Trust you will as well.

As the unfolding of what I now call Conscious Language™ continued many experiences and insights—my own and thousands of others—began to build a base of understanding, a basis of realizing the power of our Language to shape every single thing in our lives. I discovered our Language is actually our Human Operating System. I approached my upgrades with the attitude each limitation is just a set of rules believed in. These rules are a code[5], a series of Language patterns associated with memories. These memories are from my own life as well as genetic in nature. Some belief systems are so full of "Babel Viruses" they do not function at all. Sound familiar?

Have you had belief systems which were contrary to your objectives?

Upgrading our beliefs through our Language and thoughts is step one.

Our language plays a major role in our successes and our failures. I AM eternally grateful—great full, full of greatness—to God for leaving us a trail to return home and giving us a way to find home within ourselves.

The Language of our Hearts is pure, connected, already Conscious and already installed within our Heart of Hearts.

When I finally figured out we all come from our Creator's "Factory" with Pure Speech installed, I relaxed in the Faith: we have our Divine Plan awaiting our full expression. Playing our Conscious Role is all it takes to turn the stage of life into our Heaven on Earth.

Affirmations like, "I choose to consciously be in my Heart now and continuously" are very helpful.

---

[5] See the work of Dr. Bruce Lipton — www.brucelipton.com and Gregg Braden — www.greggbraden.com

I will show you what I have discovered about connecting with our Heart's Language, what our Heart's Language is and what it is, most likely, not. I share as a student. I will be able only to point you in your inner direction. You will be the only one to discover your truth, in your own Heart and give it your voice. I believe every word we speak is our prayer coming into manifestation now and now and now.

Speak only what you choose to have come into manifestation now and continuously.

"Then the LORD put forth his hand and touched my mouth. And the LORD said unto me, Behold, I have put my words in thy mouth." Jeremiah 1:9

LANGUAGE—SELF FULFILLING PROPHECY

Once I found language is self fulfilling prophecy and of the utmost importance to every aspect of my life, I started to focus on speaking only what I chose to have come into manifestation. Then the fun, upscaling and waves of transformation began.

In October, 1986, I shared my first event of my new version of Language awareness. I called it "Mastery of Words." (Eventually I called it "Mastery With Words", currently it is called "Mastery, 201 Embodying Conscious Language™.") In my first "Mastery of Words" event, about 30 of my friends, students, teachers attended. It was in the Raleigh-Durham area. The class was starting to roll along and within the first half day I found out who the class was for, me, of course.

I prepped the "students" on speaking only what they choose. How "want" meant "lack." How important it is to be first person, personal. How we were going to coach each other. They did coach me on virtually every phrase I spoke with a whole lot of gusto which my ego found somewhat (translated: hugely) challenging. They were doing a great job doing what I had asked them to do. I was struggling as they were playing back my own words and phrases for my review as fast as I spoke. "You just said 'want'." "Isn't, doesn't that mean 'is not?" "I thought we were supposed to say what is, not what is not." I just kept breathing and loving and breathing and loving.

We eventually learned how to listen until the speaker got their idea out and then coach. We were all helped with this agreement. Our active and "committed listening" required our utmost focus and attention. What an experience! I bet I learned a thousand times more through the class than they learned through me. Yes, the student is the one up in front of the class and the teachers are in the seats. I remember!

In this first Mastery of Words event, something happened which continued for two more events, until I woke up. Picture this: I was sharing how powerful language was, how important it is to be aware of each word we speak and how God, our Angels, our subconscious are all listening and bringing about whatever we say provided we say it with determination, specificity and feeling, i.e. anything Decreed.

As I was sharing these very impassioned concepts my hand waving in the air, I said, "If I was aligned with my Words and I were to say 'let there be water' then water would appear." My hand was reaching to the ceiling, pointing to an area just a few feet in front of my PA speakers, which were on speaker stands. In that very instant, the ceiling broke open and a huge amount of water poured down from some freshly burst pipes. I calmly stated "Just like that," and slowly walked over, pulled my speakers to safety, and moved a huge planter under the gushing water. The class was shocked. I was calm, poised, and matter of fact—on the outside. I asked my sound tech to please stop recording and get assistance from the hotel engineer. It took them some time to turn the water off. It took me some time to figure out what I did.

Did I get it? Not yet. We all marveled about the incident, completed the class, and they were off choosing this and that and I was off to another class, this time in York, PA. Same scenario, I started the "When two or more are gathered in My Name, I AM there" thing. This time I was being "smarter" and my decree was about the power going out. It did, in that instant! Not just a fuse or circuit breaker in the gymnasium my sponsor had rented, oh no. The whole county grid system went down for an hour. There was only a single window in the door allowing light in on ninety one of us. We were sitting there in complete silence. They were wondering if I had planned it as a joke. I was wondering if God had planned this as a wake up call to yours truly. It happened one more time. I learned my lesson.

Speaking only what we choose to have come into manifestation, moment to moment to moment, is a very good idea.

That was in 1986. I have thousands of more examples to share. Each example taught me another "good idea." What you have to continue to look forward to is waking up to your own new "Conscious Human Operating System."

As I continued to be aware of the influence of Language in my life and the lives of those I interacted with, I discovered daily the exactness of language and the connectedness of our thoughts, words, and emotions to what exists in our lives, health, finances, relationships, spiritual connectedness, and just about every aspect where words are used.

My next Scriptural upgrade came from my exploring the reference to Language from Scripture. God knew I was not going to go through a whole bunch of study on the topic, so Providence had to lend a hand. I did the same thing, you know, "OK God, I have a question in my Heart; please let me have Your answer. How about more insight on Language Dear God—You have my full attention." The next Scripture shown to me by the "open, point and read method" was the one about the horse's tongue.

"For in many things we offend all. If any man offend not in word, the same is a perfect man and able also to bridle the whole body. Behold, we put bits in the horses' mouths, that they may obey us; and we turn about their whole body. Behold also the ships, which though they be so great and are driven of fierce winds, yet are they turned about with a very small helm, whithersoever the governor listed." James 3:2-4

It took me months to begin to assimilate this statement. What did "A man who offended not in word" mean? Well, after much study and prayer, my take on this is: I AM that I AM is Pure. When we speak or think a statement using the Lord's Name in Vain, use the "I AM's" Name in vain, then we are offending our Creator; we are offending our Heart, offending Perfection within us.

"May the words of my mouth and the meditations of my heart be acceptable in thy sight, oh Lord."

By having our Language be pure, holy, clean, true, honest, blessed, blessing, clear, and definite we are using our tongues consiously and constructively. "I can't," "I am not," and "I want" are all phrases which offend the Great "I."

All these phrases start with "I," which is the "I AM."
Can our "I AM that I AM" ever "can't?"
Can our "I AM that I AM" ever "want?"
Our "I AM" IS! God is what Is.
"I am not" is impossible to our "I AM that I AM."
"I am not" is ok, for Babel and our little selves, our old self not our "I AM that I AM" Self, our New Self.
God Is Existence, Beingness, Omnipresent, Light, here and now.

"I AM the first and I AM the last; and beside me there is no God." —Isaiah 44

"I AM the LORD and there is none else, there is no God beside me." —Isaiah 45:5

Discovering my "version" of English contained hidden glitches, limiting agreements and language patterns that created separation was essential to awakening my own language of success.

> *"But I say to you that for every idle word men may speak, they will give account of it in the day of judgment." Matthew 12:36*

Every limiting language pattern reveals some new choice waiting to be made.

CHAPTER 3

LANGUAGE, OUR HUMAN OPERATING SYSTEM

Language is to you what an Operating System is to a computer. Language is our Human Operating System (HOS). Our language contains the building blocks of our reality. By adding new creative words to our Consciousness, we have expanded our capability to create. Words which offer hope, love, trust, faith, prosperity or success are words which I consider to be "Conscious." These are words we choose once we know we have a choice. Words like terror, lack, fear, distrust, struggle, and so on offer us a contracted life. I consider this language less-than-conscious, un-conscious, and limiting.

All language is creative and creates either negative or positive experiences.

The idea of our language being our operating system has helped me convey the role of language with much greater ease and clarity. As I build a new context for the role of language and the literalness of our sub-conscious mind, many new ideas may emerge within you of how you have been other than consciously creating your reality and what to do to Consciously Create what you choose.

RIGHT AND LEFT BRAIN DISTINCTIONS

Words tend to be a left brain function. Feeling tends to be a right brain function. When our language is successful and what we are saying, thinking, praying, and decreeing in words is successfully manifesting, this indicates we are using our Language (left brain) with feeling (right brain) in alignment. Understanding the qualities required for having something new happen in our life, career, relationship, finances and health is vital.

"I" is right brain. "AM" is left brain.
"I AM" is whole brain.

THE BASICS OF CONSCIOUS LANGUAGE™:

1. Speak what you choose.
2. Be first person, personal.
3. Be specific.
4. Be aligned in your feeling.

Successfully operating a computer is relatively simple. Successfully operating our lives becomes easy as we understand how we operate. To function, a computer has only a few variables. We as human beings function as a biological computer with greater complexity.

The feeling aspect, which is not in the computer dynamic, is a huge factor in having our Words become Reality. When we can be whole brain, when we can have our "I" (right brain) and our "AM" (left brain) working in harmony, our "I AM that I AM" is, or begins to be, connected and functioning.

"I" is God, "AM" is action.

At this point of our upgrade to Conscious Language™, the awakening process of our already successful "Inner Self," our "New Self" has begun or has increased. New hope and new desires will be surfacing from some stored place in our psyche.

The counterfeit of old limitation may emerge as or before our returning strength.

If we did not get it right the first time and we are still breathing, we can start again, with our new choices, our aware speaking, our Decrees.

Examples:
"I remember my good."
"I recommit to my success."
"I claim my Victory."

In delivering a new Conscious Human Operating System to our global community, I humbly know and share with you my great joy, awaiting our new upgrades and newfound strengths. Our Blessings happen because we choose them.

Our greatest weakness is
our greatest strength waiting to happen.

Life is made up of unconscious aggravations or Conscious affirmations, thoughts and Decrees.

A Decree is a Law:
Something spoken with authority
and conviction.

Take Authority and Decree:

- *I AM that I AM!*
- *I remember Pure Speech.*
- *I know and I AM my Highest Choice.*
- *I feel loved.*
- *I forgive my past creations and I AM forgiven for my past creations.*
- *I AM the Resurrection and the Life of my success.*
- *I choose to make my reboot to my new Conscious Human Operating System fun and easy.*

- *God—I AM, Light, Higher Power, Holy Spirit, Great Spirit, Christ, Buddha, Krishna, Allah. (your choice)—speaks through me and produces perfection with every word I speak.*
- *I see only perfection in myself and those I contact.*
- *I accept only Divine Truth and Wisdom at all times.*
- *I remember and embody every Divine Truth I read and Experience.*

REPORTING YOUR MIRACLES

Many years ago I gave a class in the Scottsdale, Arizona, called "Unifying Language, Imagination, Priorities, and Prosperity." I asked the class to send me their "miracles" which had to be "already realized, manifested, in hand or done." When I arrived back at my office a week after the course ended, I had already received 98 pages of miracle faxes.

Your Miracle(s) await your new choice. Your Blessings depend on Consciousness. As you upgrade to your New Conscious Human Operating System, you operate at a higher level. We operate according to the Language in our Heart of Hearts and you are initiating a change in your Language system by reading the pages in this book.

> *"Yea, my heart shall rejoice, when thy lips speak right things." Proverbs 23:16*

Focusing on, in, and from your Manifested Miracle brings it into existence, sometimes instantaneously. I love witnessing Miracles and sharing the path, process or technology which people use to attain what seems impossible or highly unlikely. Please join my Miracle Email Reporting Service and I will periodically share your stories with the rest of our Mastery Systems' Miracle Team.

Email your Miracles to: miracles@masterysystems.com. Follow this format:

- In the subject line put: Miracle Email from (your name)
- In the text message put: Your miracle. Make sure it has happened, is in your hands or is complete; not just "going to happen" or "the check is in the mail." Ensure you sharing your Victory by reporting the news instead of saying what you think is going to happen. Share from the Consciousness and reality of your goal being "complete."
- How did you do it? Let us all know exactly what word, phrase, idea, thought, or technique you used to manifest your miracle. When referencing this book, share what pages you found it on.
- What is new and different in your life now that your Miracle has happened?

Remember to be aware of your Miracles when they happen and be in the Spirit of thankfulness (full of thanks) and gratefulness (full of greatness). Remembering to write your Miracles down has them happen faster and faster. Hint, Hint.

PREPARING TO UPGRADE

> "Man's mind once stretched by a new idea, never regains its original dimension."
> Oliver Wendell Holmes

In the many courses I share, preparation of the individual and the group for their upgrades to be accomplished requires humor, enthusiasm, understanding the real benefits of upgrading, participation and lots and lots of Love. In this written form of sharing, you are the one who prepares your garden for your new "crop" of ideas, thoughts, commitments and successes. Check your body posture right now.

Make sure you are sitting as if you just won a million dollars. Our physiology can influence our Consciousness. Sit in the Consciousness and body language of success and "thrival." Neuro-Linguistics addresses this important point.

> **Insanity: doing the same thing over and over again and expecting different results.**
> **Albert Einstein**

When I first heard the definition of insanity I laughed and laughed. I laughed because I saw how true it is. Later I cried (figuratively) because I saw how much I had waited for something to change without really changing anything inside myself. I realize we have all done quite well with the operating system of the Babel Virus. Pat yourself on the back for making it this far. Your parents too. We have done well with such a huge glitch in our Human Operating System.

> **In languaging any change—any subtle change in feeling, a simple word change, a phrase change or a change in thinking—has an enormous potential influence on our lives. Changing our language changes our life "trajectory."**

My entire focus in preparing you to successfully upgrade to Pure Speech is to establish your understanding of the real role of Language in your life, the role you play in every situation you are in or will encounter.

To lighten up the whole experience, enter the upgrade process like it is a game. One-on-one Conscious Language™ Coaching can feel very challenging, like someone is being made wrong. The feeling of being made wrong is within the individual according to past memories. Since we are dealing with huge emotional patterns which most of us grew up with, playing Conscious Language™ like a game puts the process in perspective. Understanding our language patterns is neither good nor bad, they just are and we can evaluate if they serve us. If not, we can make a new choice. Here is a set of agreements to keep which make the upgrade to Conscious Language™ much easier and more fulfilling.

SUGGESTED AGREEMENTS FOR SUCCESSFULLY UPGRADING OUR HUMAN OPERATING SYSTEM

1. ***Play 125%.*** Stretch. Be willing to go as far as you think you can and then, go even farther now and now and now. As you make the agreement to be more fully present, sit straighter, breathe deeper, love more fully, show up sooner and be more alive than you ever have; your life will heal. Right now, can you focus more completely? Can you straighten your spine and breathe more deeply? Can you connect with your Inner Source more fully? Do it right now!

> You have just played 125%. The power of this agreement is to play 125% from now on. This means you have just played more fully than you ever have which translates to 100% play. Keep taking it to a Higher Level, now and now and now. Remember your agreement is to play 125%.

2. ***Live Your Word.*** Say what you mean, mean what you say, do what you say.

3. ***Be fully and completely present.*** Since Conscious Language™ is the Language of Now, being fully and completely present is a requirement to be creating in the only moment that exists, Now.

4. ***Be responsible for internal dialogue.*** Margin Note—*See page 149.*

5. ***Be effective and efficient.*** Optimize every moment... more with less.

6. ***Have a COMMITMENT to win and empower others to win,*** creating Win/Win.

7. *Give yourself permission to:*

   a. Be open to your highest good.
   b. Know.
   c. Stretch.
   d. Be enthusiastic.

8. ***Choose to choose.***

9. ***Agree to find and come to agreement.***

10. ***Be in relationship with your Inner Source.***

11. ***Stretch again and Breathe, Breathe, Breathe!***

12. ***Be committed and say "yes" to your highest good.***

Review these agreements a few times and then commit to them. If you notice you have slacked off, recommit. It may take 1,000 recommitments to transform a major challenge in your life. Are you worth it?

You are ESSENTIAL!

Thousands of successful graduates of Conscious Language™ live their lives using these simple agreements. I have seen this list on many refrigerators when visiting friends. Remember the definition of insanity, "Doing the same thing over and over and expecting a new and different result." Make a change in the way you answer your phone, speak with your spouse, play with your children, think, feel, and behave in your career and even in the way you read this book. Start now and your upgrade will already be operating.

I find great results when I create having fun with intense subjects and experiences. Our Language is much more than words in a dictionary. Our words have Creative Power and are connected to memories, feelings, thoughts, both from our ancestors and family as well as from our own life experiences. Are you still playing 125%?

THE GAME OF CONSCIOUS LANGUAGE™

1. Play your upgrade process like a game. Fun makes change happen with ease. The more fun you make your Language transitions, the more creative you will be and the faster your changes and upgrades will take place. By making this fun, our little attachments to limiting beliefs will give way to finding solutions and resolutions easily.

2. Become the Explorer into the effects words have in our lives:

- *Communicating with others*— in communicating with your family and friends, often just a simple word change brings a consistently challenging relationship into warmer and more loving interactions.
- *Communication with ourselves*—by upgrading our inner speech to a state of impeccable self empowerment, our inner world transformations reflects upon our outer world manifest reality.
- *Being communicated to*—even the way others speak to us can easily be transformed by our Conscious listening. Conscious Language™ alert us to what is really being asked for from others, what they are really feeling or what they really mean to say. Understanding others goes a long way in others understanding you.

The nature and "listening" of the subconscious mind. I believe this is one of the most important benefits of Conscious Language™. As I understand how my own feeling world interprets what I AM saying and thinking, this understanding helps me know what to do to effectively support the expansion of my Inner Consciousness.

3. Observe our current belief systems and what we have made up and proven about: God, Self, life, receiving, learning, relationships, success, feelings, work, others, money, getting things done, parents; *as expressed in WORDS!*

As an example:

- "Life is hard."
- "Life is easy."
- "Money is elusive."
- "Relationships are difficult."
- "I give to others more easily than I give to myself."
- "I have given up on success."
- "I am not good enough."
- "I have to do it all myself."

Any patterns we discover are upgradeable.

4. Explore creative alternatives in languaging, moving from the position of being right or wrong, good or bad into finding our "highest choice." However we say it is the way we have said it. It is neither good or bad, it just IS!

> "Things are neither good nor bad, thinking makes it so."
> William Shakespeare

5. Learn how to "hear" our internal dialogue and consciously "catch" and transmute it into our highest choice. The goal is to distiguish and upgrade self sabotage before it can act. And when we do, the thrill of Victory and accomplishment is exhilarating for us.

6. Be aware of "automatic unconscious speaking"—the old self—and begin to listen and speak our "New Self." Awakening to a "New Person" within us, our "Enlightened Self" is one of our great goals of physical embodiment. Our "New Self" has a Language system which is already Divine.

7. The **Formula and Chemistry** for success:

Words + Specificity + Feelings = Manifestation

Manifestation happens when you:

- Speak from your Heart
- Speak Consciously and Creatively
- Speak in first person personally
- Speak with specificity
- Speak with aligned feeling

I call this a Miracle. Miracles follow Divine Laws. It is a Miracle to me we have Divine Laws to follow.

THE CHEMISTRY FOR SUCCESS

a) *Making and keeping agreements*—Being successful means we have a measurement for success. If I do not make any agreements, I will not break any agreements. Then I will not have a way to measure my success. Scripturally these are called Covenants. Our Creator has made Covenants with us. Making and keeping our High Agreements produces our Victory.

b) *Having clear goals*—Having a goal sets our attention on what we desire. Keeping our eyes on the road allows us to drive safely. Setting goals which are clear and specific speeds up the activity of manifestation.

> "Where the attention goes the energy flows."
> Kahuna Statement

c) *Speaking our outcome*—The result of our language and the point of each interaction requires our intended outcome to have an outcome. The Babel Virus is all about disconnected, confused, confounded (not founded) language which separates us from our goals. Conscious Language™ is speaking our outcomes with specificity and feeling—Decreeing the end from the beginning.

d) *Transmuting other conflicting agenda*—Every pattern we plan to upgrade has its own agenda. It could be the agenda of struggle, lack, want, unworthiness, fear, separation, etc. As we move upscale, we realize the momentum of our old life may be directly in opposition to our newly chosen life pattern. Adjusting direction requires love and powerful guidance. As we change beliefs, we are able to easily navigate our turn in Consciousness smoothly.

> "In the province of the mind, what one believes to be true either is true or becomes true."

e) *Aligned feelings*—When words are spoken in one direction with our feeling going in another direction there is a lack of aligned feelings, and this breeds self sabotage. By speaking our desired outcome with specificity and feeling we empower our words to manifest.

8. Read this book and Upgrade your own Conscious Human Operating System in this atmosphere:

a) *Be Committed*—Take your life to a higher level—right now commit to upgrading 5 things personally and specifically in your life while reading this book.

b) *Create internal safety*—Internal safety allows limiting beliefs to surface so you can upgrade them into new options. Feeling safe is essential for our stored limited patterns to reveal themselves. Remember, many of our limitations were picked up from our loved ones. They are not bad or good. These patterns just may not serve our greatest good. Let your feeling world know Love is present as you move upscale. Nothing will be left behind, just transformed into more happiness, joy and prosperity.

c) *Supporting yourself*—Understand what may come up, as we make new choices, may be powerful and emotional. Feelings are the raw material used to build our new reality.

d) *Giving yourself full commitment*—Empower ourselves and those in our lives with our highest choices.

Playing the upgrade process in teams and families as a game helps the players feel comfortable. My Beloved wife Helena, when she was with us on Earth, would add to each class in a very loving and powerful request,

"Please, Angels, only use our material to expand Love."

Please, please remember to use the tools and techniques contained in this book to Love yourself and others more fully. It is not meant as more ammunition to judge yourself or others. Use it to Bless yourself, your family and friends.

Paul Twitchell said: *"The higher one climbs on the spiritual ladder, the more they will grant others their own freedom and give less interference to another's state of consciousness."* I echo Twitchell's conviction. Sometimes one word, when recognized and changed, will bring on a series of cascading transformations for the individual which can shake their entire known reality. Imagine helping someone realize they have been saying and believing the statement, "I want love" for 50 years. Also imagine this person makes a new choice because they realized "want" equals "lack" and they have been agreeing to "lack" love for half a century. Imagine their face as they "choose love" or "enjoy love" or "claim love" for the first time and it really happens.

The power of our Language is much more than commentary, it is Creative.

Frequently, an immediate transformation begins and in this case, the individual's world moves from "wanting" to "having" love. The change can powerfully alter our reality. Be gentle with yourself and your Loved Ones.

"A wholesome tongue is a tree of life." Proverbs 15:4

Again, be very loving and gentle with yourself and those with whom you play the game of Conscious Language™.

Remember to get permission before you ever coach anyone about their words.

The words we are using are what we currently believe to be true or we would not use them. Many of us, in the past I affirm, have been unaware of what we were actually saying and creating with our words. Many of the worded expressions we use were carved in our Consciousness through our parents and caregivers from conception on, passed lovingly on to them by their parents' parents.

I have found simply coaching myself out loud to be one of the greatest benefits to those around me. Whenever I have coached my own language in front of the class, I have helped many understand how the process of self-coaching works and that we do not have to be perfect. We can start where we are—to start our upgrade successfully.

Whatever you do, please expand Love and respect for each person's Human Operating System, starting with your own.

BENEFITS FROM CONSCIOUS LANGUAGE™

- Catch self-sabotage before it acts in your life and turn it into self-empowerment.
- Transform through language, your own areas of limitations into your heart's desires. The more diligent you are, the faster the transformation.
- Be your own optimum self-programmer; learn how your whole brain "hears" language.
- Awaken your capabilities and become a committed listening to your own inner strengths and genius.
- Turn up the volume of your "Still Small Voice."
- Instantly shift into being personally satisfied, yourself, personally. Yes, you! Personally, yeah you!
- Be in the picture and reality of your own success.
- Be your own partner in health. Discover how your health is directly influenced by your languaging.

- Immediately adjust your states of lacking to your choice of having, being, doing, enjoying, and thriving.
- Have fun coaching your self into your victory, over and over again.
- Learn how close Spirit is, in every breath.
- Know the difference between process and outcome. It is the difference between "working on getting something" and "having something."
- Understand sarcasm (translated—sarc—the tearing of flesh) for what it is.
- Develop a whole brain approach with specificity—words (left brain) and feeling (right brain).
- Effectively communicate your ideas while simultaneously accessing creativity, receptivity and understanding in your life.
- Discuss challenging topics while remaining focused and productive.
- Support your team, family, company, relationships, or organization to get on track quickly and stay on track.
- Provide your children, family, and friends an effective joyous operating system in their own mind, feelings, and experience.

CHAPTER 4

THE PLAYING FIELD—CONSCIOUSNESS

Consciousness is what we are aware of being.

LANGUAGE SHAPES CONSCIOUSNESS

When we hear a new word and understand its meaning, our Consciousness is altered and expanded. Imagine a family who grew up never seeing an ocean or knowing of the existence of an ocean. Once they are able to grasp the concept of an ocean, their awareness would be greatly changed.

Believing the world was flat was a given only a few hundred years ago. Traveling too far in the ocean in the flat planet consciousness was setting yourself up for falling off the planet. Many of the beliefs we hold true today may give way to a greater truth as we continue to live and experience life. Our children have an entirely different reality than we have even though we all eat at the same dinner table.

Language defines our reality.
Language shapes thought.
Thought shapes reality.

Wanting is a state of lack. To want is to desire without having. Want is one of the upgradeable words. What we replace it with will change our consciousness. "I want love" is a very common phrase. "I want more money" is a very well-used phrase. I did not know every time I said "I want" I was agreeing with wanting or not having. When I woke up to what the word meant is when I woke up to being able to make a distinction between wanting and having. "I have love" is very different than "I want love." Say them both. Which feels better to you?

Much of what will transpire through this book will be shifts in your experiences through shifts in your language.

It is important to test every idea shared in these pages and find what works well for you. The nature of language is very deep for each of us. To offer new options for Languaging is a very humbling and sacred responsibility in my life. If you were sharing with me such an important topic as thoughts, words, and feelings, I would desire to know where you are coming from, how you use it, and if you were trustworthy for me to even listen to. If we were in person, you would have my eyes, tone and body language to be with and make a determination on if I AM trustworthy.

Since we have this book for now, I will give you some of my personal approaches or beliefs about life right up front. If you have different views, honor them. I do. Put scripturally, *"Prove all things and hold fast to that which is good."*

OUR LAUNCH PAD OF CONSCIOUSNESS

Here are my beliefs and suppositions from my life experiences related to this upgrade called Conscious Language™. I give simple explanations and expansions when supportive to help clarify my views and beliefs. Many books in our world's libraries discuss, in depth, the various views on the role of the individual in co-creating their experience of life. My focus in this treatise is to share systematic upgrades to Consciousness through Conscious Language™.

- *We co-create our experience of our reality*. When a life event happens, our attitudes and feelings toward our experience will determine whether we move upscale, downscale or stay static.

- *We give power to our experience through our attention.* Example: Focusing on problems reveals problems. Focusing on solutions brings solutions.

- *Where our attention is, so are we.* Worrying about lack breeds more lack. Focusing on others' limitations puts us in the consciousness of limitations. "Seek and ye shall find."

- *Energy follows thought.* Fighting for peace is like making love for virginity. Peace is attained when we are at peace in consciousness. Saying, "I don't know" only breeds "not knowing." Choosing to know brings knowing.

- *What we put our attention upon we become.* Driving at a high rate of speed requires the driver to keep their eyes on the road. Looking to the right or left usually turns the automobile in that direction. Keeping our attention on our goal is essential to winning our goal.

- *The subconscious mind is literal.* Tell yourself "I can't" and your subconscious will keep you in can't. Say "I can" and mean it and watch miracles happen.

We have been using a language system of Babel—confusion—dating back centuries. And mostly we have been using it unconsciously, until now.

> The thing always happens that you really believe in; and the belief in a thing makes it happen.
> Frank Lloyd Wright

- *Consciousness returns consciously.* Wishing some subliminal tape—talking to our unconscious self— will help us become conscious is an ineffective way to be personally and consciously responsible for our reality. On the other hand, waking up and being aware of what we are saying and what each word means will produce a powerful return to Consciousness.

- *Only when we are aligned with our words, i.e. have Faith do they "happen."* "Faith is the substance of things hoped for, the evidence of things unseen."

- *Language is our operating system,* shaping our thought and reality as specifically as a set of blue prints defines the architect's ideas to the builder.

- *Language is either conscious*—aware—*or unconscious*—unaware.

- *Language is creative.*

- *Words are spirit vibrating into reality.* The alteration of one word can change an entire reality.

- *When we know the name of a thing* we have power over the thing. As I discover the operation of my speech I have the power to take authority and re-author my speech and my reality.

- *Only when we are prepared emotionally, spiritually, mentally, and physically will we transform one reality or condition into another.*

- *All change starts in Consciousness first.*
- *Our language is to our lives as software is to our computers.*
- *Death and Life is in the power of the tongue.*
- *We have the power to change our thoughts, words and feelings.*
- *We are exactly what we are Conscious of Being.*
- *Changing our Consciousness is the first step of changing what we are conscious of Being.*

In exploring our Human Operating System and upgrading it to our Conscious Human Operating System, it helps to have our awareness and commitment engaged. As a human consciousness, our awareness is how we function. Our "computer" of consciousness must be in the "on" or "aware" or "learning" position to upgrade.

STATES OF BEING AND LANGUAGE PATTERNS

Each state of awareness will have common language patterns supporting the state of consciousness we find ourselves in. By having awareness of the influence of each word or worded expression, we have the ability to determine if our language and belief is serving our Highest Good or if we will benefit from changing our belief system.

Vagueness

Being vague is being committed to not having something specific. Vagueness is safe to limited beliefs because it does not require any actual data for manifestation. Specificity brings up feeling. Feeling is the key to healing. Stay vague, stay out of focus and your dreams will only vaguely almost happen. Be specific, be in focus, and you will start Consciously manifesting. You will also start feeling.

Despair

Despair is also "not-paired" with your choice. When we are in despair we are feeling disconnection (un-paired) with our goal. Despair is a signal to pair or repair. All despair will have some worded expression tagging along which separates the individual from their desire. Example: "I have no one."

Lack

Lack is a belief in not enough or being separate from the thing desired. Not enough is impossible to I AM that I AM. Language coupled with conscious choice turns lack into abundance quickly.

Struggle

Struggle is the easy way to give power away. I can say "This is a struggle" or I can say "I choose to make this fun and easy." It takes just as much energy to say or believe either phrase. The fun and easy choice releases more energy for your use. The struggle phrase is a lot more difficult just by definition.

Co-dependence

We can base our happiness on others or we can share our happiness with others. Happiness is up to us. Having our happiness dependent upon others approval puts them in control of us. Time to upgrade.

Ineffectiveness

Effectiveness is a strong belief in our capability. Babel breeds ineffectiveness. Making a new Conscious word choice initiates an immediate change in effectiveness. Just making a new choice can upgrade our success rate. To boost effectiveness, get personal. Being specific is powerfully effective.

Cold Communications

Old hurts have a way of engaging survival. When enough hurt is present the individual can opt—usually unconsciously—to "not care anymore." Coldness is a survival pattern based on fear. These experiences are real to our emotional bodies and take great care and lots of love to transform. For those who are cold, find out what past hurt is feared. Fear is not a good master. Choose to heal the hurt into comfort and transform fear into confidence and courage. Be willing to be intimate again. Trust will heal coldness. Love will heal all unto itself.

Settling

If a building's foundation settles it weakens the entire building. Surrendering to less than your Dream, to acquiesce, to accept less than you deserve or believe possible is settling. Babel supports settling. Settling is a belief in our dreams being outside of us. Settling is being unwilling to change the situation. Conscious Language™ is an operating system of connection and remembering our Creator within, our Heaven within. Thriving is so much more pleasing than survival and settling.

Making do

"Making do" can be very positive and effective. It can also be a form of settling. Check your levels of joy and fulfillment to discover which you may be doing. Being resourceful by making do can be very creative as long as you keep on choosing and manifesting your Heart's Desires.

Choosing only what is reasonable or possible

When we choose only what seems reasonable or possible we are defining a state of acceptance of the illusion, limitation, or lack. We will justify our "reasons" as real yet the bottom line is we are not using our true Imagination or Creative Ability to create our chosen outcome. This became very clear to me in my Imagination Activation Courses.

Running a four minute-mile used to be unreasonable until someone did it. Now it is the standard. Are your dreams unreasonable? Good, because you will have to think outside the box of reasonableness and limited possibilities and explore the miracles which are here for you through your thoughts, words, and imagination.

"With God, all things are possible."

Feeling Disassociated

Disassociation is another direct result of Babel language. Speaking first person, personal, conscious, creative, and outcome-oriented language changes this state in a hurry. "The money" turns into "My money."

Health Challenges

My interactions with individuals and their health conditions led to my awakening to the deep role of language as a creative force in our lives. Every health state will have some direct or indirect language pattern—hidden until you realize what you are saying— underlying the condition. By waking up to language and its role in our health you will have powerful understanding about what you have been thinking, feeling, and saying in relationship to your health. Your health is upgradeable. "A man who offendeth not in word, the same is a perfect man and able to bridle the whole body."

Financial Challenges

Health and wealth are sisters. Our "I AM" self contains—and is one with—all health and wealth. Babel is the virus of separation which confuses our understanding of our union and oneness with our Creator and all Creation. Conscious Language™ effectively upgrades lack into abundance. "When ye pray, ask, believing ye receive and ye shall receive."

Relationship Challenges

The mirror of relationships most certainly reflects back to each of us our own inner disharmonies and harmonies. As we upgrade to our Heart centered communication system, relationships heal and unify powerfully and quickly.

Family Disharmony

Blame, shame, stating what not to do, vagueness, Co-Dependence, and statements like "I feel like" and "I feel that you should" can be easily upgraded to functional communication between family members. State what you feel. "I feel sad and I choose to feel joy..."

Not knowing how

When we ask ourselves how to do, have, or be something, we enter a state controlled completely by language. "Choosing to know" how to do, have, or be something immediately changes our brain state. Our new choice upgrades our previous limitation to allow for knowing, doing or having. Language is a power activator of reframing patterns. Our genius and innate intelligence is accessed through our thoughts via language.

> **You are the only one who controls your thought. You are the Co-Creator of your world.**

Unconsciousness

"I don't know" is in operation in the state of unconsciousness. Choose to remember! Remember means to "be one again re-member, re-one, re-unify, re-connect.

Unaware

Consciousness and awareness are the same. If you walk out and reach into your pocket and notice your keys are not there, do you say, "I forgot my keys?" The truth is you just remembered your keys! Awareness an unconsciousness are focuses shaped by our common everyday language patterns. "I am not aware" can easily be upgraded to "I choose to be aware." We are authoring our lives with every thought and every word. Aware people are at the top of the success ladder.

Discomfort

When a person says "I feel uncomfortable" they are saying what they do not feel. "Un" is not. Babel, as you will discover in the following pages, is great at saying what is not (isn't). If I respond to a question about how I feel, I can state how I do feel. Instead of discomfort I could say "I feel a little cramped and I choose to stretch." Stating what is and how we do feel is placing us in creative mode and putting us in the present—now. God is a God of what is! I AM is God in Action! Light IS!

Keep your language about what is!

Depression

The opposite of depression is expression. When my wife and life partner passed on, I slowly became depressed. I asked myself what did depression turn into and my Heart answered, "Expression." I realized I had become depressed by holding back my expression to my loved ones about Helena's transition because it was painful. My depression lifted the very moment I began expressing to my loved ones.

Depression is waiting for expression!

Shame and Guilt

These two patterns are all about blaming or shaming ourselves through the thoughts of others. We are the ones who attract or subconsciously create the perceived judgment from others because we have not dealt with self-judgment within ourselves. Conscious Language™ powerfully addresses, through language awareness, personal responsibility and choice. Turn shame and guilt into self-honor and self-respect.

Resentment

Resentment is re-sent judgment and anger. Forgiveness and forgetting the matter is the only way to stop re-sending the judgment or the resistance to a perceived judgment. By forgiving, we stop the back and forth pattern. Love is the only energy stronger than resentment. Do it, you will like it!

Hate

Hate is massive Love inverted. In hate the individual once loved immensely. Transforming hate many times takes paragraphs of Conscious Language™ to restore the energy into immense Love again. If hate is present a huge amount of Love is waiting to be restored.

Each one of the experiences within these states has very specific language patterns common to the state. By understanding our language as a shaping quality of our life experiences, we alter our experience by shifting our language. It takes will and awareness to shift our Language.

The more aware we are of language patterns and what to turn each pattern into—through our conscious choice—the more dynamically powerful we are in moving upscale through limitations into successes.

Being aware of our Human Operating System helps to bring to Consciousness the power of our thoughts and words upon manifestation. Knowing we can learn or install a new Conscious Human Operating System is very inspiring to those committed to thriving.

UNCONSIOUS HUMAN OPERATING SYSTEM COMPARED TO CONSCIOUS HUMAN OPERATING SYSTEM

UHOS	CHOS
Reactive	Active
Suppressed	Expressed
Resists Authority	Effective authorship
Sorting outside	Sorting from inside
Mental based	Heart based
Diminishing life	Increasing life
Energy is decreasing	Energy is increasing
Relationships moving further apart	Relationships becoming closer & more intimate
More justification	More realization
More blame	More blessing
Less effective	More effective
Looking behind	Looking ahead
Living what isn't	Living what is

THE NATURE OF LANGUAGE

Language: shapes our reality, focuses and directs energy, defines and gives boundaries and is literally accepted by the subconscious mind.

Language is the medium of our thought. Thought is the medium of our reality. Changing our language medium "can" change our thought which "potentially" changes our REALITY.

"As a man (woman) thinketh in his (her) heart, so is he (she)."

"POSSIBLE" COMPONENTS OF THE MIND

The Subconscious Mind:

- is power without direction
- receives direction from the conscious mind—anyone's conscious mind
- plays back what it receives like a computer
- is literal
- responds to repetition
- responds to feeling
- attracts experiences to us according to our beliefs
- is always operating and functioning

The Conscious Mind:

- has power of choice
- has freewill to direct or be directed
- can create unconsciousness
- can suppress into or express from the subconscious at will

The Super Conscious Mind:

- gives us 100% of the information in the conscious and subconscious mind, which is our Reality

For many years, I shared Conscious Language™ in my "Mastery" courses. As a result of reading Michael Gerber's book *The E-Myth*[6], I realized from his writing and trainings, the importance of creating a "system".

---

[6]E—Myth by Michael Gerber, Harper Collins 1996 — 2001

I prayed and Decreed to find a system for helping my community wake up to Conscious Language™. While resting in the sun I drifted off to sleep and received "the system." Upon waking I immediately wrote down, as fast as I could, an outline of what later became the system explained in Part B of this book. Systems I created allow me to share in a more effective and empowering way.

Let us enter the world of a new language, a new operating system—the Conscious Human Operating System—using Conscious Language™ and discover our personalized version.

> *"In a dream, in a vision of the night, when deep sleep falleth upon men, in slumberings upon the bed; Then he openeth the ears of men and sealeth their instruction."*
> *Job 33:15—16*

SECTION B

THE DOMAINS OF LANGUAGE

(Gates of Consciousness)

I have named my "system" The *Domains of Language*. Systemizing our words into groups with common qualities greatly helps Conscious Language™ students "remember" with ease. Thank you, Michael Gerber!

I invite you to enter the Domains of Language like you would a mythical land where the battle of dark and light is waging and you are essential in tipping the scale. Imagine you are finding for your first time the awareness and techniques you require to free yourself, your family, your company, and loved ones from some limiting "spell"—because you are! Imagine you have received an ancient text which describes an all powerful sword which you discover is the spoken word.

It is up to you, and you are the only one who can free you, which frees everyone. I AM here discovering with you. Every Human Life Stream is here. Some are aware they are here. You are here and you know many others who are aware or will be "remembering" how to upgrade Babel into Pure Speech. You will find, as I AM, this story is very real and essential for the fulfillment of the Divine Plan. You will discover your WORD is your sword of LIGHT, your sword of LIFE.

YOU ARE ESSENTIAL and play a very important role in this story called LIFE.

CHAPTER 5

DOMAIN OF LIMITATION AND NO CHOICE

This is the first set of self-sabotage words I discovered. When upgraded a whole new life starts for the individual.

> Say out loud: "I want love."
> Now say: "I have love."
> Then say: "I choose love."

Say each statement over and over and let your feelings let you know the difference between each phrase. The Domain of Limitation and No Choice is by far the most easily identifiable because it is the bottom rung of the Babel ladder. It is usually the Domain people didn't know they were in because they did not realize what the words mean or what they are saying or that they have a choice. "Wanting" and "having" are direct opposites. I will give you the Domains in order of my discovery. The Domain of Limitation and No Choice is what turns this ship around.

> **A change from want to choose is going from reverse and death into forward and life.**

"...choose you this day whom ye will serve;" Joshua 24:15

EXAMPLES OF THE DOMAIN OF LIMITATION AND NO CHOICE

Statement ➡	**Consequence**
I *want*	Want means Lack
I *need*	Need is without
I *can't*	I can not
It's *too hard*	Not just one hard, two hard
I *don't know how*	I do not know how and I can prove it!
I come up with a *blank*	And I am not going to fill in the blank, so there.
I run into a *wall*	Ouch!
I'm *blocked*	And I can prove it!
I'm *numb*	And the "b" is silent, the way I like it
It's *beyond my control*	So don't blame me!
It's *out of my reach*	So don't ask me to stretch
I *don't undesrtand*	And they can prove it

Our subconscious mind says: "Ok" and is obedient to our words.

Results of the Domain of Limitation and No Choice: Our creativity is blocked or limited and real choice is denied.

Note: What is a choice, a conscious choice? Many people over the years have said, "Since I have it in my life, I must have chosen it." We create it, yes! If it is not our highest choice, it is not a real "choice." It is just a manifestation of some limited belief. Anything less than love is less than choice.

Anything less than our highest choice will contain self-sabotage.

The Domain of Limitation and No Choice blocks choice by decree. By saying "want" we are agreeing to be in "lack." We all have the opportunity to hear ourselves say a limited statement and believe it or make a new choice. Consciousness is being aware of what we are saying and, if it is not our highest choice, making a new choice. *We are designed to thrive!*

"The Lord is my shepherd, I shall not want." Psalms 23:1

This is very clear. If the Lord, The Law, The I AM is my Shepherd, then I can do all things through Him, God, I AM, Christ, Higher Power. Wanting is not in the picture unless I decree it so. When I say, "I want" I am confirming "I am desiring without having." If I say "I desire," I am being aware of an urge to have, do, or be something yet to be or not yet manifested in my experience. It is a calling forth. "I choose" is even more powerful. Desire has meanings like "of the father" or "of the stars."

Want *equals* lack.
Can't *equals* can not.
Need *equals* requiring without yet acquiring.

These words represent a powerful state of limited Consciousness and can be healed on our planet and in our Hearts by making a new choice today! Now! This very instant!

Imagine having all of us from conception through our full life, being awake to having and enjoying our Hearts' desires continuously.

What we do right now blesses generations to come. When does the promised thousand years of peace and plenty begin anyway?

Now is the only time that exists.

UPGRADE EXAMPLES TO THE DOMAIN OF LIMITATION AND NO CHOICE

Limitation	Upgrades to
First Say	Then Say — OUT LOUD
I want	I Choose. I Claim. I Have. I Empower myself to have. I Will have. I AM claiming. I Deserve to have. God in me can. I enjoy having …
I can't	I Can. I Choose to be able to. God in me can. I Empower myself to be able to. I will find a way to be able to. Will you help me do this?
It's too hard	I Choose to make it ease. I Empower it to be easy. Even though it appears challenging. I will do it.
I *don't* know how	I Do know how. I Choose to know how. I will find out how. I AM within me knows how ...
I come up with a *blank*	I fill in the blank with my choice. I AM creative and come up with an idea...
I run into a *wall*	I move through all obstacles. My way is clear. I find my way...
I'm blocked	I AM clear. I have my clear path. My Divine way is prepared. I AM the open door...
I'm *numb*	I feel. I sense. I choose to feel. I transform my numbness into sensitivity. I experience …
It's *beyond* my control	It's within my control. I have Divine control...
It's out of my reach	It is within my reach. All I require is at hand now. I contact and have all I require...
I *don't* understand	I Choose to understand. I do understand. Please help me understand...
I *need*	I Choose. I Claim. I Have. I Empower Myself to Have. I Will Have. I AM Claiming. I Deserve...

Note: Find or create the upgrade phrase which you are most aligned with and feel deeply. To have our words happen, your feeling, specificity and alignment are the key. *Want* is one of our biggest global Consciousness shifts. *Wanting* and separation are sister states. *Wanting* is a state of lacking. When we are one with our Creator and our Creator is within us, then how could we want for any good thing? I have heard many ministers say, "God wants you. "Please, lovingly let your minister friends or spiritual leaders know to make a new choice and move from teaching "want" to teaching having, being, and receiving.

> *"If any of you lack wisdom, let him ask of God, that giveth to all men liberally and upbraideth not; and it shall be given him." James 1:5*

The Domain of Limitation and No Choice upgrades into the Domain of Opulent Choice.

> "Everything you can imagine is real."
> Pablo Picasso

Stay diligent with your upgrades. Catching and changing every want will surely have a profound influence on your life. I remember one beautiful grandmother taking the class in the 80's who discovered she had been "wanting" her husband of forty years to change a behavior. She woke up to the fact her "wanting" was an agreement to be without the change and her husband was going along with her "want" by not changing. She made a new choice right there in class. The next day she came to class and announced her husband had "changed" automatically. She was on cloud nine and looked twenty years younger. How did this happen so easily? "Decree a thing and it shall be established unto you." Choosing something is very powerfully positive. Wanting something is powerfully limiting. What is your new choice in your life?

QUICK REVIEW

- Say your upgrades OUT LOUD. Let your body hear your new choice. Say until you feel it in every cell of your body!
- Change "I want" into "I choose," "I have," "I claim," "I AM." Find the words which you are fully aligned with which are positive and creative.
- Be creative and Conscious, stating what you do choose.
- Transform limitation into your ever expanding good.
- Gather a group of family and friends and practice Conscious Language™ together
- Play your upgrade like a game and make it fun and easy.
- Coach yourself and teach by example.
- Speak with feeling, specificity, and alignment until you feel the meaning in each word as you say it and it happens.
- Imagine you are speaking to unruly children—thought forms—and authoritatively directing them to where you desire them to go—your Heart's highest choice.

CHAPTER 6

DOMAIN OF NON-CHOICE

As we move up the Conscious Language™ ladder, the Domain of Non-Choice is a simple and often hidden way for our limited beliefs to stay limited. I call it re-booting Babel while we think we are making a Conscious choice. It is like a computer virus taking over our computer behind the scenes. It seems safe to open a file but underneath the sinister activity of the virus is about to run its destructive code. Each domain becomes more and more subtle the further we go up the Conscious Language™ ladder. I have found our job is to become more and more aware, and speak only what we choose. What ever your Spiritual path may be you will discover you become more and more Concious with every upgrade.

> *"Seek ye first the Kingdom of Heaven and its righteousness and all else shall be added unto you."*

EXAMPLES OF THE DOMAIN OF NON-CHOICE

Carefully phrasing your choice is of utmost importance. The table below shows how what could be Conscious and creative language turns into what "is not" or states what is "not desired."

Statement ➡	Consequence
I choose to...*(this part sounds good, however...)*	*not be sad*—not be *equals* death, like "not being here anymore" *not* be fat—die fat *not* struggle—get knotted up while struggling *not* be poor—die poor not do that again—and again and again
I choose to...	*lose* weight—so I can find it again and again *stop* struggling—struggle with struggling *quit* smoking—start again so you can quit again and again *never* do that again—and again and again

Subconscious Mind Says: "Ok" and provides more sadness about not having, not doing, not being or remains stymied about what to do, since it is incapable of "not" doing something. We are beings of what is. Our minds and energy are constantly creating something.

Not being or losing is blocking our Life Force.

Results of the Domain of Non-Choice: Not having, not doing, not being.

Note: As we move upscale and understand what a real decree or choice is—a new level of value is self assigned by the individual to every word, and ultimately every thought. The Domain of Non-Choice is all about what isn't. It is focusing on stopping or quitting something. If I say, "Don't think about pink elephants... with purple poka-dots flying from your left to right before your face," do you anyway?

Telling our children not to be late makes them focus on exactly what we do not desire. Ask them to be on time or in by a set time. Remember to say what you do choose! We are upgrading much more than just words when we move to Conscious Language™. We are upgrading our Consciousness and our "Reality."

UPGRADE EXAMPLES TO THE DOMAIN OF NON-CHOICE

Non-Choice	Upgrades to
First Say	Then Say — OUT LOUD
I choose *to not*	I Choose to
…*to not* be sad	I Choose to be happy
…*to not* struggle	I Choose to make it easy, to enjoy Grace
…*to not* be fat.	I Choose to be fit, thin, healthy, wear a size ___ dress, pant, shirt, etc.
…*to not* be poor.	I Choose to be wealthy, abundant, have ___ amount of money and be abundantly supplied with money as fast as I require it now and continuously…
…*to not* do that again.	I Choose to do __________ (state what you do choose to do, continuously…)
I choose to: *lose* weight.	I Choose to be fit and comfortable in a size _____ dress/pant…
stop struggling.	I Choose to start enjoying ease about _______
quit smoking.	I Choose to be a fresh air breather,…
never do that again	I Choose to consistently do what is successful,…

The Domain of Non-Choice upgrades into the Domain of True Choice.

By making choices, Conscious choices, we admit our role in the process of manifestation. Choice is the bottom line for any successful person who has overcome something. We can be controlled by the limitation or we can make a new choice. Knowing how to make a Conscious Choice through Conscious Language™ is like the computer programmer knowing the "right language" or the "right code" to accomplish the required task. Our subconscious is literal and awaits our choices.

> "High thoughts must have high language. "
>
> Aristophanes

The more personal,
the more specific,
the quicker the action.

QUICK REVIEW

- Say your upgrades OUT LOUD. Let your body hear your new choice. Say until you feel it in every cell of your body!
- Choosing to "not be" results in something starting to "die." "Not Being" is not existing.
- Losing is in opposition to success. All life is to win—win—win.
- Stopping energy takes more force than directing energy.
- What we put our attention upon we become.
- Say what you do choose.
- We are beings of what "is" because we "are." State what is or what you are committed to have, do, or be. If any limitation shows up, it is asking for upgrading into your highest choice.
- All creation, being created, can be recreated by our Consciousness.

CHAPTER 7

DOMAIN OF INEFFECTIVE CHOICE

A typical example of the Domain of Ineffective Choice, is political correctness and socialization. They are particularly active in attempting not to be too direct in order to not offend someone else, and by being politically correct we can "make everyone happy." This pattern is very effective at being ineffective. A very high level commitment is required to upgrade ineffective choice into effective choice.

EXAMPLES OF THE DOMAIN OF INEFFECTIVE CHOICE

Statement ➡	**Consequence**
I'll *try* to do well.	Trying is only half a commitment, our subconscious only knows how to do, not try.
I *hope* it will work.	Leaves the possibility of failure. For example: "Honey will you marry me?" "I hope so." Do not expect wedding bells with that answer!

Statement ➡	Consequence
I *intend* to improve.	Intend is try with more letters. "Honey will you marry me?." I intend to" Oops! Not too strong a commitment, eh?
I'll *attempt* to change.	Another form of try.
Have it happen, I *think*.	"Have it happen" is solid. *"I think"* second guesses and weakens the strength.
Perhaps I can do it.	Try with more letters. What does "per-haps" mean anyway? Pure Babel!
I'll *kind* of make it.	I kind of hope you can kind of make it because I kind of would like to maybe have you kind of show up, maybe! Babel at its finest.
I'll *possibly* do it.	No commitment
I *almost* have it.	I know what "all" means and "most" means, what does almost mean? Somewhere between everything and lots of everything.
I *would like* to choose.	"Would like to" is only a future possibility. "Honey, will you marry me?" "I would like to choose…" No wonder people pretend to get married for a little while until they would not like to continue anymore.

Our subconscious mind says: "Does not compute," either does it or not, says yes or no, starts or stops, and opens or closes.

Results of the Domain of Ineffective Choice: No action, no result, energy is activated and not directed or only "attempted."

Note: Upgrading the Domain of Ineffective Choice means we become effective, present, and our subconscious self begins to listen. A whole host of new experiences transpires when the student takes the horns of this Domain and becomes determined to be functional and successful.

UPGRADE EXAMPLES TO THE DOMAIN OF INEFFECTIVE CHOICE

Ineffective Choice	Upgrades to
First Say	Then Say — OUT LOUD
...*try* to do well	I do good, I AM good, I do well, I choose to do good ...
...*hope* it will work	It works, It will work, I work it well ...
...*intend* to improve	I commit to improve, I AM improving ...
...*attempt* to change	I do change, I AM changed, I commit to change ...
...have it happen, *I think*	I do have it happen, It does happen, I experience it happening ...
...*perhaps* I can do it	I can do it, I AM doing it now, I do it well for sure...
...*kind* of make it	I do make it, I make it now ...
...*possibly* do it	I do it, I AM committed to doing it now ...
...*almost* have it	I have it, I AM committed to having it now, I enjoy having it ...
...*I would like to choose*	I choose to do it, I AM committed to doing it now ...

The Domain of Ineffective Choice upgrades to the Domain of Effective Choice.

> "The great enemy of clear language is insincerity. When there is a gap between one's real and one's declared aims, one turns as it were instinctively to long words and exhausted idioms, like a cuttlefish spurting out ink. "
>
> George Orwell
> *Politics and the English Language*

Political correctness and the Domain of Ineffective Choice have a lot in common. A successful organism must first know who or what it is before it can expand. I test each phrase with a simple question like, "Honey, will you marry me?" "I would like to" is not a great response. It does not effectively answer. Becoming effective and definite requires a strong sense of "self" and will propel the speaker into making certain what is so.

QUICK REVIEW

- Say your upgrades OUT LOUD. Let your body hear your new choice. Say until you feel it in every cell of your body!
- Try, Hope, Intend, Perhaps, and Attempt are wimpy words.
- Trying is impossible to our "I AM" and our subconscious mind.
- A computer does not know how to try. Same with our "inner operating system;" it only does.
- Instead of being politically correct, be powerfully direct.
- Stress is increased by trying and attempting.
- As you drop the phrases of the Domain of Ineffective Choice you will already be more effective.

CHAPTER 8

DOMAIN OF ABSOLUTES AND GRANDIOSITIES

In this arena of language, a very specific pattern is revealed. The Domain of Absolutes and Grandiosities (DAG) expressions reveal the vagueness and improbability of absolutes while giving clues to the emotion of suppressed grief. The "always, totally, everyone" comments we make reveal a deeper need not to get specific, because specificity brings up feeling.

The more specific we are,
the more instantaneous the manifestation.

Since specificity is so very important to manifestation, the DAG plays a major role in both feeling and specificity. If you find yourself hanging around this Domain, check yourself for some suppressed grief or sadness you may be avoiding. Sadness and grief, when felt with love, turns into joy.

EXAMPLES OF THE DOMAIN OF ABSOLUTES AND GRANDIOSITIES

Statement ➡	Consequence
...*always* be better	Better in Egyptian Frog Hair Weaving? Vague.
...help *everyone*	Have you met everyone yet?
...better in *everything*	How will you measure betterness in everything?
...complete *transformation*	Become a frog? No, still a living thing, therefore not a complete transformation. Death? No, we are still energy.
...totally *improve*	Total is the absolute state connected to a vague level of bettering.
...*absolutely* get it	Another total word which takes another total word to describe "completely" for "absolutely" perfect understanding.
...*perfectly* obtained	Define perfectly. Another absolute and may be too vague.
...the *best* I can do	Could you have done better?
...giving it my *all*	When we give it our all, there is nothing left.

Our subconscious mind says: "HUH?" "Say what?" Who is everyone?" What does complete transformation mean?

Results of the Domain of Absolutes and Grandiosities: Vagueness, incompleteness, foggy concepts of absolutely nothing...

UPGRADE EXAMPLES TO THE DOMAIN OF ABSOLUTES AND GRANDIOSITIES

Absolutes and Grandiosities	Upgrades to
First Say	Then Say — OUT LOUD
...help *everyone*	Help who specifically? The more specific, the more powerful the statement, the deeper the feeling.
...*always* be better	Better in what way specifically? Better or effective, successful in what way exactly?
...better in *everything*	Better in what specifically? Attaining what exactly with what specifically?
...complete *transformation*	Transformation into what specifically?
...totally *improve*	Improve how specifically? Improve what specifically?
...*absolutely* get it	Get what, in what ways specifically?
...*perfectly* obtained	Obtained how, in what way specifically?
...the *best* I can do	I did it specifically how? In what way? I did a great job!
...giving it my *all*	Giving it my full focus, my enthusiasm, my commitment.

The Domain of Absolutes and Grandiosities upgrades into the Domain of Specificity.

Getting specific takes courage, clarity and exactness. Divinity is in the details. Have you ever seen a vague flower? No, just very specific simple or complex flowers. Not vague.

"By your words you shall be justified and by your words you shall be condemned." Matthew 12:37

> "If we spoke a different language, we would perceive a somewhat different world. "
> Ludwig Wittgenstein

The Domain of Absolutes and Grandiosities corresponds to the Scale of Emotional Harmonics which I introduce later in this book[7] . When specificity is lacking and absolutes and grandiosities are present, grief and sadness are frequently being suppressed. You will be able to discover, usually within three words or less, what suppressed emotion is present.

I have found a correlation between Emotion and Language which is very helpful in coaching myself and others into our Heart's Desires. At first the student of Conscious Language™ may find themselves speaking less. With practice you may find yourself becoming more and more articulate and specific—Decreeing each choice Word by Word.

QUICK REVIEW

- Say your upgrades OUT LOUD. Let your body hear your new choice. Say until you feel it in every cell of your body!
- Absolutes and grandiosities are too big for our Conscious Mind to comprehend, therefore when we use absolutes and grandiosities we tend not to get results.
- Grief and sadness are hidden in absolutes and grandiosities.
- Getting specific brings up feelings.
- Feelings are avoided in absolutes and grandiosities.
- Sadness and grief, when felt with love, turns into joy.
- Practice getting first person, personal, and specific with your choices and watch your deep feelings return. Also watch your power to create return.

---

[7] See page 150

CHAPTER 9

DOMAIN OF CONDITIONAL CHOICE

This is the "strings attached" domain that unknowingly until now, set up a series of conditions through our consciousness, shaped by our tongue, where one thing must happen before another can happen. I lead a training using the common phrases found in the examples of the Domain of Conditional Choice in which we discover our other than consciousness commitments. Take your time with this Domain and find powerful keys to unlock repeating limitations and blockages which seem to come out of the blue.

EXAMPLES OF THE DOMAIN OF CONDITIONAL CHOICE

Statement ➡	Consequence
I choose to be good so *that* I will be loved.	The only way love shows up is if you are good.
I'm going to look smart to *be* accepted.	Acceptance only happens if you look smart.
I'm committed to success *in order* to have my dad love me.	Dad will only love me if I achieve success.
I like to smile *so* others will like me.	Others like me only when I have a smile.
I'm going to join a fraternity because it will make me look popular.	If I do not get in the fraternity I will not look popular. The only way I can get popular is if the fraternity lets me join.

Our subconscious mind says: "Ok" and sets up a condition where one thing must happen prior to, or simultaneously with, another thing happening.

Results of the Domain of Conditional Choice: One condition can be met only after the other condition.

UPGRADE EXAMPLES TO THE DOMAIN OF CONDITIONAL CHOICES

Conditional Choice	Upgrades to
First Say	Then Say — OUT LOUD
I choose to be good *so that* I will be loved.	I choose to be good *and* be loved.
I'm going to look smart *to be* accepted.	I'm choosing to be smart *and* be accepted.
I'm committed to success *in order* to have my dad love me.	I'm committed to success *and* I'm commited to having my dad love me.
I like to smile *so* others will like me.	I like to smile *and* have others like me.
I'm going to join a fraternity *because* it will make me look popular.	I'm joining a fraternity *and* I choose to be popular.

The Domain of Conditional Choices upgrades into the Domain of Clear Choice.

The power of *And Consciousness* is wonderful. It allows both states or conditions to happen in any order without being conditional. I choose happiness and love and my wealth and my Divine Partner and doing what I love to do and... The addition of the word *and* opens the door for any order of manifestation or all manifestation at once. *And Consciousness* is what shapes Creation.

Look at what our Creator is creating all at the same time! The birds and the bees and the flowers and the trees and the Moon up above and...

The word *because* is misunderstood. If I say, "I am happy because you love me, I have set a condition—codependent on being happy. Explore using the word *because* as two words: Be and Cause. Then by Being Cause or being first cause in our lives, we Decree a thing and it is established unto us.

QUICK REVIEW

- Say your upgrades OUT LOUD. Let your body hear your new choice. Say until you feel it in every cell of your body!
- Conditional Choices are very frustrating because they set arbitrary conditions on one thing having to be present before another can happen.
- Connecting our choices with *And Consciousness* allows freedom of the Divine Plan to happen in any order.
- I choose love and happiness and joy and abundance and health and victorious financial success and our peaceful planet. *And* is a wonderful connector.

CHAPTER 10

DOMAIN OF THE THIS, THAT, THESE, THEY, THEM, THOSE, IT, THE

Discovering the Domain of the T's woke me up to finding and having real connection in my life. My students find, as I do, changing one word, many times one of the T's, brings instantaneous change from separation to connection. Go slow with this power Domain and allow the upgrades to be assimilated deeply within yourself. Merge with each new phrase until you experience your Inner Self saying "Yes."

EXAMPLES OF THE DOMAIN OF THIS, THAT, THESE, THEY, THEM, THOSE, IT, THE

Statement ➡	**Consequence**
I choose …	
to have *the* son I've always hoped for.	*The* son, *the* body, *the* wife, *the* husband, *the* family, *the* job—all impersonal and detached.
to receive *this* help.	*This* support, *this* understanding. When we use the word *this* it makes the listener search for what is being referred to from a former comment.
to be *that* friend.	*That* is separation, like that car, *that* family.
to share *these* gifts.	*These* may refer to last year's birthday gifts.
help from *those* friends.	*Those* may refer to Aunt Martha's friends.
to have what *they* have.	*They* may refer to the hogs in the pen.
love from *them*.	*Them* may refer to bed bugs.
to have *it* for my relationship.	*It* may refer to varnish remover.

Our subconscious mind Says: Not enough information to act. "Who specifically?" "What specifically?"

Results of the Domain of "T's:" Vague, nonspecific, unconnected, impersonal, implied, therefore no action taken or the Consciousness has to review words which have gone before to determine which statement or individual or idea, "This, That, These, They, Them, Those, It, The" referred to, vastly slowing down communication or making clear communication unstable and open to interpretation.

UPGRADE EXAMPLES TO THE DOMAIN OF THIS, THAT, THESE, THEY, THEM, THOSE, IT, THE

T's	Upgrades to
First Say	Then Say — OUT LOUD
I choose ...	
to have *the* son I've always hoped for.	*my* son, *our* son.
to be *that* friend.	*your* friend, *my* friend, *our* friend.
to share *these* gifts.	*my*—*your*—gifts.
to receive *this* help.	*your* help, *my* family's help.
the help of *those* friends.	*my* friends, *our* friends.
love from *them*.	from who specifically?
the support they are.	*you* are or who is specifically?
to have *it* for my relationship.	have what?

The Domain of the T's upgrades into the Domain of Ownership.

Getting connected with your chosen outcome in your life happens in the upgrade of the Domain of the T's. Ownership is essential in manifestation.

Speak these words out loud and feel the difference.
"The family?" Whose family? "My family."
"The money." "My money."
"The Planet." "My Planet."
A world of change happens the instant we become personal.
"The war" turns into "our war."

When individuals and nations become personal, commitment to change happens much faster.

In my courses students frequently upgrade one word from the Domain of the T's and remember their forgotten childhood. What happens to you when you go from "The Family" to "My Family"? Please take your time and assimilate these new word synapses. New connections will be established when you feel the meaning in each new word or phrase deeply enough.

SAY THE FOLLOWING OUT LOUD:

My money.	My love.	My home.	My Heart.
My children.	My spouse.	My finances.	My job.
My back.	My body.	My health.	My God.
My Prayer.	My Dreams.	Our family.	Our Planet.
Our parents.	Our children.	Our community.	My success.

Do you notice a deepening of your experience? Conscious Language™ is speaking first person, personal, conscious, creative, outcome oriented, and outcome producing language with feeling and specificity. *This, that, these, they, them, those, it, and the* are impersonal and support separation.

The Domain of T's upgraded establishes our direct connection to our lives here and now, personally.

QUICK REVIEW

- Get personal.
- Be in your picture.
- Claim your position to your choice.
- Own your choice.
- Connect with your vision through My and Our and being specific with Who, What, Where, When.

CHAPTER 11

DOMAIN OF CANCELLATION

In the Domain of Cancellation we find words that negate part or all of what we have just said. The words and phrases in this domain serve as "take backs," making it possible to express contradictory thoughts in one sentence. I call this domain pure Babel.

The subconscious mind responds to words and phrases in the Domain of Cancellation by starting and stopping itself from taking action. It essentially ends up back-tracking each step it takes. This one-step forward, one-step-back motion results in people feeling oddly out of sync with what has been said.

EXAMPLES OF THE DOMAIN OF CANCELLATION

Statement ➡	Consequence
I'm excited, *but*	*But* cancels I'm excited.
You did a good job, *however*	*However* cancels You did a good job.
I love it, *although*	*Although* cancels I love it.
Won't it be great?	*Won't* it means Will not. Won't it be great? means Will not it be great. Answering Yes will be saying yes it will not be great.
Don't you enjoy that?	*Don't* means Do not. Don't you enjoy that? means Do not you enjoy that?
Isn't it beautiful?	*Isn't* means Is not. Isn't it beautiful? means Is not it beautiful?
Doesn't it look excellent?	*Doesn't* means Does not. Doesn't it look excellent? means Does not it look excellent?
Shouldn't you come early?	*Shouldn't* means Should not. *Shouldn't* you come early? means Should not you come early?
Wouldn't you like to go?	*Wouldn't* means Would not. *Wouldn't* you like to go? means Would not you like to go?
Didn't you love it?	*Didn't* means Did Not. *Didn't* you love it? means Did not you love it?
Can't you help?	*Can't* means Can Not. Can't you help? means Can not you help?

Our subconscious mind says: "Yes, not."

Results of the Domain of Cancellation: The statement cancels itself.

UPGRADE EXAMPLES TO THE DOMAIN OF CANCELLATION

Cancellation	Upgrades to
First Say	Then Say — OUT LOUD
You did a good job, *however*	You did a good job *and*
I'm excited, *but*	I'm excited *and*
I love it, *although*	I love it *and*
Won't it be great?	It *will* be great.
Doesn't it look excellent?	It *does* look excellent.
Isn't it beautiful?	It *is* beautiful.
Shouldn't you come early?	*Please* come early. Are you coming early?
Can't you help?	*Can* you help? Please help.
Wouldn't you like to go?	*Do you* choose to go? Will you enjoy going?
Didn't you love it?	*Did you* love it?
Don't you enjoy that?	*Did you* enjoy that?

The Domain of Cancellation upgrades into the Domain of Confirmation.

> The meanest, most contemptible kind of praise is that which first speaks well of a man and then qualifies it with a "but."
>
> Henry Ward Beecher

For those who love to empower others with your communication, pay very special attention to the Domain of Confirmation as the upgrade to Cancellation. By adding *And Consciousness* and being direct and confirming, communications become empowering, fun, and effective. Instead of "n't" each other, we directly affirm each other or ask questions directly. "Ask and ye shall receive." And Consciousness is more like Divine Consciousness which is free to create or co-create according to our Heart of Hearts. The Domain of Cancellation is a great example of Babel and how it confuses our tongue and mind, limiting us in ways which were previously hidden.

QUICK REVIEW

- Say your upgrades OUT LOUD. Let your body hear your new choice. Say until you feel it in every cell of your body!
- Eliminate the contractions—n't.
- Ask direct questions like: "Are you," "Can you," "Will you."
- You "And" instead of "but," "however" and "although."

CHAPTER 12

DOMAIN OF PROCESS WITHOUT OUTCOME

Constant and continual processing and working on something does not mean a positive result or outcome will happen. Have you ever found yourself or a loved one working on an issue instead of resolving the issue into a result? Have you noticed yourself being in the doing phase of life instead of the Being phase of life?

Most dis—ease comes from this Domain. To understand who we really are and what we are capable of requires creating an outcome with each commuincation. Ask yourself: "What Am I creating with my words?"

Are we human doings or human beings?

EXAMPLES OF THE DOMAIN OF PROCESS WITHOUT OUTCOME

Statement ➡	Consequence
...*change* my life	*Changing* anything does not define an outcome.
...do it *differently*	*Differently* is vague and does not give the required information for someone else or our own Inner Self to act.
...*adjust* my income	*Adjust* again is vague. Up or down?
...*transform* my relationship	*Transform* is only a process and does not state what the transformation forms into.
...*alter* my plan	*Alter* only varies something. Vague.
...in the *process* of therapy	Double the trouble. *Process* is a process word. Therapy is also a process word. This statement is being in the process of process.
...*working on it*	And *working* on it and working on it. Does not state an outcome, only the process of working on it. I am working on being forgiving does not forgive.
...*dealing* with it	*Dealing with* issues is like playing cards. I have two griefs, two angers and one self-righteousness, what do you have? Go fish. Also, *dealing with* problems does not invite the resolve, the solution.
...it's *starting* to make a difference	Another double. *Starting* is a process, making a difference is also a process, a vague process.

Our subconscious mind says: "OK, OK, OK, all right already!"

Results of the Domain of Process without Outcome: Constant and continual processing without the desired outcome.

UPGRADE EXAMPLES TO THE DOMAIN OF PROCESS WITHOUT OUTCOME

Process w/o Outcome	Upgrades to
First Say	Get Specific — OUT LOUD
...*change* my life	How specifically, in what way, shape or form? Feeling what, seeing what, experiencing what specifically?
...do it *differently*	*Differently* how? What exactly is different? What is the new result or outcome? Who will benefit exactly? What are the new distinctions?
...*adjust* my income	In what way? Up or down? By when? By how much? In what time frame?
...*transform* my relationship	Into what?
...*alter* my plan	How specifically, in what way, shape or form?
...in the *process* of therapy	How specifically, to attain what? What is your goal for therapy? What is your therapist's goal? To heal what into what?
...*working on it*	Working on what to attain what? What is your outcome?
...*dealing* with it	To attain what outcome specifically?
...it's *starting* to make a difference	For what specific purpose? Finalizing in what destiny. What are the new differences specifically?

The Domain of Process Without Outcome upgrades into the Domain of Fulfilled Outcome.

With focus and follow through, you can direct your thoughts and words into exactly what you are choosing, fulfilling your desire instead of just moving energy toward it. Would you rather deal with a problem or have a solution? Would you rather work on something or attain something? Would you rather start to make a difference or have a new state exist?

See the end from the beginning.
Speak the end from the beginning.

"I have declared the former things from the beginning; and they went forth out of my mouth and I shewed them; I did them suddenly and they came to pass." Isaiah 48:3

QUICK REVIEW

- Say your upgrades OUT LOUD. Let your body hear your new choice. Say until you feel it in every cell of your body!
- Include the result of any changing state.
- See the end from the beginning.
- Be the Omega from the Alpha.
- Define your change into what exactly and specifically.
- Work on it or have it?
- Deal with it or change it into something?

CHAPTER 13

DOMAIN OF CO-DEPENDENCE

When Helena and I became aware of co-dependency as something to heal, we dedicated ourselves to learn what was available for us to move upscale. Helena ordered every book on the subject from our book supplier. We noticed processing was common in Co-dependence support materials and what was missing was Conscious connected outcomes.

We realized Conscious Language™ played an important role in upgrading co-dependence. The application of Conscious Language™ provided important clues to help heal this state.

Our version of the definition of co-dependence: "In relationships, whenever our happiness is dependent upon another person, place, condition or thing and if even that person, place, condition or thing is present or signaling it is OK to be happy and we are not."

Ultimately, happiness comes from within.

Anytime our happiness comes from outside instead of from inside ourselves, co-dependence is present. I—along with many authors on the subject of co-dependence—believe everyone, to some degree, is co-dependent.

What does this *approval addiction* turn into?

In our systematic approach to what I call the Tools and Technologies of Mastery, each limited state becomes healed or upgraded into a healthy state. The dis-ease heals into some form of ease. The lack state turns into some form of abundant state. The depression state turns into some expression and so on.

Co-Dependence turns into co-Empowerment.

In our system the ideal is to upgrade every reaction into positive action. Co-dependence shows the "co" meaning more than one is involved. Co-dependency is about our relationships. Healthy relationships are co-empowered and harmonious relationships.

In addition to finding your own word patterns which may be co-dependent, you can ask yourself the following:

- Do you say "Yes" when you really mean "No?"
- Are you consistently aware of what others are thinking and feeling while you feel unsettled or fearful you may be the cause of some upset?
- Do you always check in with others about what they desire without checking in with yourself first?
- Even if you are doing for others, do you feel empty yourself?
- Are you indirect or vague when describing your needs or choices?
- Does bringing up something which will rock the boat stress you out?

EXAMPLES OF THE DOMAIN OF CO-DEPENDENCE

Statement ➡	Consequence
I am happy *if* you're happy.	Others control our happiness.
You *make me* angry when you do that.	That is probably true, if others control us.
It's my parents' fault that I have problems with intimacy.	True as well, if we like giving our power away.
I hope *I can make you* happy.	And I hope I can take a breath.
I *couldn't* go to college because I had to raise my children.	Puts the blame and responsibility on your children.
Let me go to the bathroom.	No… well OK…
Let me think.	No, like I can control your thinking.
I've got to resolve this so you'll feel better.	Pure co-dependence.

Subconscious Mind Says: "OK" and gives its power away.

Results of the Domain of Co-Dependence: Perpetual disempowerment and sublimation to the will and choices of other person or persons.

UPGRADE EXAMPLES TO THE DOMAIN OF CO-DEPENDENCE

Co-Dependence	Upgrades to
First Say	Then Say
I *am happy if* you're happy.	I AM happy and *I empower you to be* happy. Happiness is our own responsibility. Claim it for yourself and then "bless" others with happiness from your own happiness. If you are going to help someone from drowning, first be able to swim yourself.
You make me angry when you do that.	*I Experience* anger when you do that. Owning what we feel is establishing healthy boundaries. First we will know who we are before we will be able to find our own happiness with ourselves and ultimately w ith others.
It's my parent's fault that I have problems with intimacy.	*I picked up* challenges with intimacy through my perception of my parents. Own your situation and you have power to change it.
I hope *I can make you* happy.	I choose to be happy and *I empower you* to be happy. I enjoy happiness. Hoping is a weak position. Making someone else happy is an illusion. Sharing in happiness is the strongest possibility. By being happy, I AM in a better position to share my happiness with someone else. Having my happiness dependent upon my ability to make another happy gives my power away to another's state of life.
I *couldn't* go to college *because I had* to raise my children.	*I chose* to raise my children instead of go to college. Whether we chose our situation or just allowed it, we ultimately "created" or "co-created" it. By owning it, we take authority again and can begin to author our lives. Say "I couldn't" do this or that only has our "I" self in a state of limitation. We create it, we can recreate it.
Let me go to the bathroom.	*I AM going* to the bathroom. One of the funniest things for me is to hear myself or another adult say "let me go to the bathroom." This pattern must be left over from some kindergarten classroom bathroom experience. If someone says this phrase to me these days, I usually say "No" and watch their response.
Let me think.	*I AM thinking...* Wow, what power we give away with this statement. As if someone can actually have such control as to allow thinking for another person. Many of the adepts and sages would have loved to be told not to think so their mind could be clear, present and in the state of Now.
I've got to resolve this so you'll feel better.	*I AM committed* to feeling resolve about this, what about you? As you may have noticed, words like "I've got to, I have to, I must" are compulsion and motivated by fear. Many times Co-Dependence contains qualities of worry and fear of not being loved if something is not just so and so.

The Domain of Co-Dependence upgrades into the Domain of Co-Empowerment.

Imagine being so confident in yourself and secure in your own choices and requirements your energy field is well established and clearly defined. This is also a description of healthy boundaries. Imagine you clearly communicate with others because you are clear within yourself, exactly what you choose to say, do, be, have, and receive.

Those who have mastered Co-Empowerment are fun to be with because you know what to expect and exactly where they "are" in consciousness. Being direct, specific, and first person, personal in Languaging goes a long way to healing co-dependency.

"Thou shalt have none other gods before me." Deuteronomy 5:7

QUICK REVIEW

- Fulfill yourself and others will be calm in your presence.
- Own your state of existence.
- Communicate your requirements.
- Be clear on your requirements.
- Empower others with being fulfilled.
- Instead of needing others to be happy so you are happy, share your joy with others.

"The entrance of thy words giveth light; it giveth understanding unto the simple." Psalms 59:130

CHAPTER 14

DOMAIN OF IMPERSONAL DISCONNECTION

(Formerly called Specific Quality without Personal Connection)

In the Domain of Impersonal Disconnection we encounter words with positive meaning and promise; yet, the words exist apart from any personal connection and remain as vague ideas. The Domain of Impersonal Disconnection is the epitome of sounding great with no action to follow up the great sound. The reason for this is the phrases and statements in this Domain do not carry enough information and specificity to direct Creation to manifest anything specifically.

The subconscious mind does not respond to the words of the Domain of Impersonal Disconnection until specificity is added. Please realize you are close, very close, to your outcome in the Consciousness of Impersonal Disconnection. Now get personal and get connected!

EXAMPLES OF THE DOMAIN OF IMPERSONAL DISCONNECTION

I choose...	Love Support Happiness Joy Victory Empowerment Completion Prosperity Consciousness

The subconscious mind says: "OK, how, with whom, in what way, how often, when, where, still searching, more data please."

Results of the Domain of Impersonal Disconnection: Energy is mobilized yet does not land because the destination is not identified.

Every single coaching I have been involved in or witnessed addressed the upgrade of this Domain at some time. The degree of specificity and connectedness is the degree or level of information the Universe or God or "I AM that I AM" uses to produce manifestation.

In the following suggestions for upgrading the Domain of Impersonal Disconnection, allow yourself to fill in each blank with your own personal choices and watch miracles happen in your life.

Take your time; be intimate, honest and real. You may be one single word away from miracles happening in your own life.

UPGRADE EXAMPLES TO THE DOMAIN OF IMPERSONAL DISCONNECTION

Impersonal Disconnection	Upgrades to
First Say	**Add specifity**
I choose...	
love	With whom, in what ways, shapes and forms, how often, feeling what, healing what, for how long, establishing what specifically in your life, from whom?
support	With whom, in what ways, shapes and forms, what type of support, giving you what experience, empowering you with what, from whom, how specifically, awakening what within you, to do what?
happiness	With whom, in what ways, shapes and forms, about what specifically, enjoying what exactly, in what situations, for how long, blessing who?
joy	About what, with whom, in what ways, shapes and forms? Healing what into what specifically?
victory	In what ways, experiencing victory over what, in what? Changing which appearances of defeat into what victory? Changing what in your life specifically?
empowerment	From whom, in what ways, specifically? Empowering who to have, do or be what specifically? Empowerment of what into what specifically?
completion	Of what, when and how specifically? Completing what and benefiting how exactly?
prosperity	How much, when, feeling what, enjoying what specifically? Freeing you from what into what specifically?
consciousness	With whom, in what ways, shapes and forms? Aware or conscious of what exactly, benefiting how specifically?

The Domain of Impersonal Disconnection upgrades to the Domain of Connected, Personal Outcomes.

QUICK REVIEW

- Have your outcome be personal.
- Be specifc in your communication.

CHAPTER 15

DOMAIN OF OUTCOME, ALMOST

In the Domain of Outcome, Almost—the goal is so very close. This language pattern usually goes undetected, appearing good enough for those who do not really choose to have their success, partner, acknowledgement, and happiness. If they get specific, feelings will happen. Babel is a trickster and loves to influence us to think we are there. Of course there is never here. Go the extra mile for your own victory! Bring your outcomes here and now! Be specific and personal.

EXAMPLES OF THE DOMAIN OF OUTCOME, ALMOST

...love with my father
...support from my employer
...happiness with my spouse
...increase my income 10 percent
...empower myself
...heal the disease

Our subconscious mind says: "OK, I can begin, and more data is required for completion."

Results: Energy directed and connected without specific action, time, place, event, memory, etc.

UPGRADE EXAMPLES TO THE DOMAIN OF OUTCOME, ALMOST

Outcome, Almost	Upgrades to
...love with my father...	What type? Experiencing what? Sharing What? Healing what specifically?
...support from my employer...	What type? In what form? To experience what specifically?
...happiness with my spouse...	How? In what ways? Enjoying what specifically?
...increase my income 10%...	By when? By how much, how often?
...empower myself...	In what specific way and in what situations?
...heal the disease...	Into what? Feeling what? Having what change specifically? Into what state of health specifically?

The Domain of Outcome, Almost upgrades into the Domain of Outcomes Fulfilled.

We are on our way to bringing our words, thoughts and feelings into a new state of Consciousness and a new state of Reality. By going a few more steps up the Consciousness ladder within ourselves, our very thoughts, shaped by our newly emerging connected Conscious Language™ birth our Dreams into Existence.

Our Heaven on Earth begins. Please invest in your well-being in real time, NOW.

QUICK REVIEW

- ✓ Who?
- ✓ What?
- ✓ Where?
- ✓ When?
- ✓ With whom?
- ✓ How often?
- ✓ Personally!
- ✓ Here!
- ✓ Now!

CHAPTER 16

DOMAIN OF CREATIVITY AND OUTCOME

In the Domain of Creativity and Outcome words are precise, personal, passionate and powerful. Communication is clear and easily understood.

People in the Domain of Creativity and Outcome are accustomed to having their hearts' desires. They speak personally, specifically and with feeling.

The subconscious mind responds to the language spoken in the Domain of Creativity and Outcome by manifesting people's desires easily and quickly.

EXAMPLES OF THE DOMAIN OF CREATIVITY AND OUTCOME

I *have* love.	Be personal and specific.
I *AM* loved.	Be personal and specific.
I *come from* having, doing, being.	Be personal and specific.
I *empower* myself to have, do, be.	Be personal and specific.
I *claim*.	Be personal and specific.
I *imagine* having, doing, being.	Be personal and specific.
I *give myself permission* to have, do, be.	Be personal and specific.
I *appreciate* having, doing, being.	Be personal and specific.

Our subconscious mind says: "OK!" "Yes!"

Results of the Domain of Creativity and Outcome: Manifested desires come easily and quickly.

Understanding and noticing automatic responses, which initiate the creative process, is our first step in upgrading to our New Conscious Human Operating System. The upgrade process is mighty and is best approached with determination and conviction. The more Spirit filled you are about your upgrades, the greater the conviction and Faith you have to transform the illusion of limitation into your reality of Opulence and Plenty.

Stay with your upgrade until you feel your words in every cell of your body. Say it until you get it!

The Domain of Creativity and Outcome is designed to get your connected creative juices flowing. The Domain of Language of Mastery is designed for our inner Master Self to have full authority. Study the words of Scripture. What a great example for us to model.

"Thy word is a lamp unto my feet and a light unto my path."
Psalms 46:105

"But I say unto you, That every idle word that men shall speak, they shall give account thereof in the day of judgment. For by thy words thou shalt be justified and by thy words thou shalt be condemned."
Matthew 12:36—37

CHAPTER 17

DOMAIN OF MASTERY

THE LANGUAGE OF MASTERY

In the Domain of Language of Mastery the frequency is very high and personal responsibility to be Conscious is at the forefront of our focus and attention. I AM is our strongest statement of being. I AM that I AM rings true for every person I have had the opportunity to be in the Presence of.

> *"And God said unto Moses, I AM THAT I AM: and he said, Thus shalt thou say unto the children of Israel, I AM hath sent me unto you." Exodus 3:14*

By having an agreement to speak consciously, creatively and only what we choose to have exist; we open up a new set of linguistic links to our Heart's desires already fulfilled. By practicing the statements in the Examples of the Domain of Mastery (and these are only examples) we train ourselves to have each response to our life situations be conscious and creative; automatically. Being automatically conscious is the outcome of embodying the Domain of Mastery.

THE LANGUAGE OF MASTERY—VERSION 1

I Can
I AM
I Will
I Choose
I Have
I Love
I Create
I Enjoy

Our subconscious mind says: "Yes, I can, yes I AM…!"

Results of the Domain of Mastery: Manifested desires come easily and quickly.

People in the Domain of Mastery are accessing their creativity, their choice, their Hearts quickly and effectively. Listening to and being with an individual who speaks Language of Mastery with confidence is very reassuring.

Imagine our business and industry leaders operating on Language of Mastery. Imagine our educators, governmental leaders, health care practitioners and environmentalists thinking in Language of Mastery, where *can't* and want have been upgraded to *can* and *choose*.

Say *I Can* silently and powerfully for an entire day. Watch your life transform. Watch your world around you begin to reorder itself around your new confident stand for your *I Can* state of being.

Do the same with I AM. I AM is God in Action. I is God, AM is action. Give "I AM" statements to yourself for one hour. I AM is our source code of existence. I AM is the frequency which created and sustains us, each of us.

When you do your *I Will,* make your statement one of using your "I AM's" will. A simple way to check yourself is to say I Will, God Will, *I Will,* God Will. The idea is to have your "I" and you word for "God" be equal in feeling. In each statement "I" is representing our I AM Self.

I Can, I AM, I Will, I Choose, I Have, I Love, I Create, I Enjoy becomes a prayer or mantra to focus our Inner Presence on being successful.

The subconscious mind responds to the language spoken in the Domain of Mastery exactly as you say it. If you say I Can your subconscious believes you—as long as you feel what you say and continue to feel the meaning in what you say long enough to have it exist in your reality.

"For it is not ye that speak, but the Spirit of your Father which speaketh in you." Matthew 10:20

If you say *I can't,* usually you say it like a matter of fact and you can't. Use the Domain of Mastery as *statements of fact.*

Mean what you say! Say it until you feel it! Say it until everything opposing your statement gives way to your good.

"But whoso keepeth his word, in him verily is the love of God perfected: hereby know that we are in him." 1 John 2:5

UPGRADE TO THE LANGUAGE OF MASTERY—VERSION 2

I AM
I Can
I Will
I Choose
I Have
I Love
I Create
I Enjoy

"Be still and know that I AM God." *Psalms 46:10*

I AM goes first. Depending on where you are in your Spiritual evolution, "I can" may be your first lead off, as you are remembering. "You can do all things through Christ who strengthens me."

Leading off with "I AM" quickens the results and frequency as the "I AM" is fully experienced and understood. God is very personal. God is so One with us when we are using "I AM" statements; I invite you into your own experience by using your own Conscious "I AM" Statements.

Every Word we speak is the Spirit of God—our Breath being shaped into Words by our Consciousness. This is why it is essential to speak only what we choose to have come into manifestation now and continuously.

> *"Thou art snared with the words of thy mouth, thou art taken with the words of thy mouth."* *Proverbs 6:2*

SECTION C

CONSCIOUS LANGUAGE™ APPLIED

CHAPTER 18

THE LANGUAGE OF MASTERY

Distinguishing between the Domain of Conscious Creative Language and the Domain of Mastery

Ultimately, the sincere student works actively in the Consciousness of these two very powerful and transformative Domains. Over the years, through my own life's experiences and the lives of other students of Conscious Language™ an important challenge of alignment and believability began to emerge in our approach to upgrading to Conscious Language™.

> "High thoughts must have high language."
>
> Aristophanes

As we discovered limiting language, especially being spoken unconsciously about something of vast importance to us, the immediate response was to jump into the "right" words to make it all better. Usually based on fear the automatic correction only compound the issue.

As we chose to be more successful in our careers or upgrading our income streams, we said something like:
"I really want to get on with it"—frequently we would over compensate and say a new "right" word like:
"I choose to get on with it" or
"I am getting on with it"—missing what our subconscious was asking for.

Check in with all your worded expressions and realize they are coming from some place within you, deep within you. They may be genetic—coming from your lineage—or experiential—coming from your experiences. The key is to be aware and feel what you are saying. If you notice an upgrade is required, make sure you deeply feel your upgrade. Saying the right word in no way makes it happen.

Saying what you deeply feel, saying what you are committed to and saying your Heart's top priority is the key!

Using the Domain of Conscious Creative Language moves things in the right direction. The Language of Mastery is essentially the Domain of I or "I AM." To function, this Domain requires us to feel the meaning in each word *fully and completely.*

Say out loud:

"I come from having love."

Then say:

"I AM love."

Notice which statement you feel most aligned with, grounded in and which is clear and definite. Conscious Language™ works when we are first person, personal, specific and feel the meaning in each word with alignment.

Do the same (out loud) for the following:

I *empower* myself to have love.	I *have* love.
I *claim* my wealth.	I *AM* wealthy.
I *appreciate* having my health.	I *enjoy* my health.
I *give my self permission* to find my Divine partner.	I *love* my Divine partner.

The first statement in each of these four lines is from the Domain of Creativity and Outcome. The role of this Domain is to initiate, start, and engage a new direction, new choice, and new result. Sometimes the DCO will work and we are off and running with great happiness because we "chose right."

The second statement in each of the four lines is from the Language of Mastery. This Domain goes direct! There is not a lot of preparation and getting ready and claiming; just Being, 'Can'ing and 'AM'ing. If the second statement is too much, then use the DCO statement until you can go to the LOM statement.

The successful use of Conscious Language™ happens when we realize our thoughts manifest through our Language; when we say what we mean or when we say what really matters to us.

Using the higher levels of Conscious Language™ requires our being Conscious of each word we speak. Using the "I AM" statements effectively and meaningfully brings about a very powerful and Spirit-filled state.

> **Be willing to find whatever works for you from exactly where you are in your current reality and keep making your Prayer, Affirmation, Choice, and Decree until what you say happens.**

> *"...speaking the truth in love, may grow up into him in all things, which is the head, even Christ."* Ephesians 4:15

I understand more fully each day the conversation of my Inner Man and the dying of my outer man. When I first started using Conscious Language™ in 1986, choosing was the most important thing as an upgrade. I knew what not to say, just not how to recreate my reality. As time went on and I had the opportunity to work with thousands of other sincere students of Truth, I began to witness many of us using the "right" words and still not getting results every time.

Our awareness was shifting to be aware and positive, yet some worded expressions were just not delivering the goods. I have discovered we were not, at that time, really changing our Consciousness enough for the new state to appear. Language being prophetic—*"the word becomes flesh"*—means we are prophesizing with our words, but only when certain factors are present.

Please read the following carefully!
It is a story about Consciousness—it is everyone's story!

> [18] *I will raise them up a Prophet from among their brethren, like unto thee and will put my words in his mouth; and he shall speak unto them all that I shall command him.* [19] *And it shall come to pass, that whosoever will not hearken unto my words which he shall speak in my name, I will require it of*

him. [20]But the prophet, which shall presume to speak a word in my name, which I have not commanded him to speak or that shall speak in the name of other gods, even that prophet shall die.

[21]And if thou say in thine heart, How shall we know the word which the LORD hath not spoken? [22]When a prophet speaketh in the name of the LORD, if the thing follow not, nor come to pass, that is the thing which the LORD hath not spoken, but the prophet hath spoken it presumptuously: thou shalt not be afraid of him." Deuteronomy [18-22]

Let us explore this idea further and relate it to our own lives. "I will raise them up a Prophet from among their brethren, like unto thee" brings the question, who is the "thee" spoken of?

When we read the scriptures from the standpoint:
"The Kingdom of Heaven—Kingdom of God—is within"
and / or
"Christ is within you"
and / or
"I AM THAT I AM"
then reading scriptures becomes a process of awakening.

Speaking, praying and activating our "I AM" state within us makes every word we think, speak, and feel more personal, Divine, and Creative. To have a word happen, it requires landing on good soil within our Consciousness.

[21]And if thou say in thine heart, How shall we know the word which the LORD hath not spoken? [22]When a prophet speaketh in the name of the LORD, if the thing follow not, nor come to pass, ***that is the thing which the LORD hath not spoken,..***

So, if it happens, the Lord has spoken.
Where is the Lord?
What is the Lord's Name?
I AM is the Lord's Name.

When I say "I AM" or "I Can" or "I will," I AM using the Name of the Lord. And when I say "I can't," I am using the name of the Lord—I AM—in vain.

Prove all things and hold fast to that which is good.

A Conscious Language™ upgrade means we become Conscious with our words.
Saying it right does not mean Conscious .
Say it until it happens in our Consciousness!

Creation happens first in Consciousness before or as Creation happens in our outer world.

Being Conscious of the word "plenty" does not mean we have plenty existing in our own Consciousness. The bank might have plenty or your rich Uncle Pete might be Mr. Plenty, yet actually identifying with plenty happens when we are conscious of "I AM plentiful," "I have lots of money," "I invest with ease", "I AM prosperous." Our "I" or "I AM" is in the picture. Plenty comes from within!

Affirm Out Loud:

- I love having lots of money.
- I receive money with ease.
- Wealth is my natural state.
- I AM supplied by my Great I AM Self.
- My wealth increases daily.

Also Decree with Feeling:

- I AM conscious of my wealth.
- I AM conscious of God supplying me now and continuously.
- I AM conscious of my businesses continual success.
- I AM conscious of being Conscious.
- I AM conscious of World Peace.
- I AM conscious of my Happy Family.

Find phrases which actually change your Consciousness. Move from desire to ownership. The whole platform of the first event of our Core Curriculum at Mastery Systems is to find the words already in our Heart and say them.

Conscious Language™ is something we use to help us remember the Truth in our Hearts.

I AM That I AM is within us. Pure Speech is the expression within us, from our Heart and is recognizable because it happens as we say it. It is the Lord—within—speaking or prophesizing through us. I have witnessed this thousands of times.

"Decree a thing and it shall be established unto you."

"A man who offendeth not in word, the same is a perfect man and able to bridle the whole body."

"Life and death is in the power of the tongue."

"In the beginning was the word, the word was with God and the Word was God."

God is Consciousness.
We were created by the Word.

"And the Word was made flesh."

Every Word we speak is a Prayer or Decree coming into manifestation moment to moment. By learning what we are actually saying when we speak—silently or out loud—we can evaluate if what we are saying is what we choose to Prophesize.

As we get our intention and commitment aligned, speaking only what we choose to have come into manifestation, our energy follows thought and our Inner Man (Woman) begins to grab hold of our tongue and Consciousness and Miracles begin to happen.

[6]*Therefore my people shall know my name: therefore they shall know in that day that I AM he that doth speak: behold, it is I." Isaiah 52*

[24]*And it shall come to pass, that before they call, I will answer; and while they are yet speaking, I will hear." Isaiah 65*

[10]*...let the weak say, I AM strong. Joel 3*

FROM SELF-SABOTAGE TO SELF-SUCCESS

I humbly and enthusiastically share with you a Truth I have discovered in my study of Conscious Language™ and the power of the Word in Manifestation.

Our Word, being Spirit Declared, goes forth to do what is Declared. Declare only what you choose!

With the faith of a mustard seed, we have been given the responsibility to issue our Decree in full confidence it is accomplished by the very issuing of the Word. If we follow our thought with some subtle sense we must take some action to get our Word to happen, we have broken our Covenant with our Creator.

"What things so ever ye desire, when ye pray, believe that ye receive them and ye shall have them." Mark 11:22-24

I have found this idea to be the underlying Truth in successful "I AM" Conscious ministers, healers, grandmothers, grandfathers, moms, dads, and all those who believe their prayers are answered.

> "Those who restrain desire, do so because theirs is weak enough to be restrained. "
> William Blake

To insure your Declaration is a Decree in the Highest Order, make sure your statement is in accord with your Heart, including only your Highest Choice—not settling. Make sure your Decree is something you are aligned with having, doing, being or sharing and Blesses all Life through its Manifestation.

Yes, a new car can fit these requirements. Any statement which is qualified with the feeling—Conscious or unconscious—of want will bring your outcome with you still being in the state of wanting, even though you physically have it. Your fervent prayer, qualified with wanting, can bring a new car to your neighbor so you can continue wanting it. How many of us or those we have known have wanted to be married, only to get married—seemingly—and still *want* union?

Living the path of Conscious Language™ is much more than saying it "right." When you Speak, Pray or Decree, make sure you trust your Creator Loves you enough to honor your request and will, by the very belief, "ye receive," will *acquire* what you *require.*

> "The great enemy of clear language is insincerity. When there is a gap between one's real and one's declared aims, one turns as it were instinctively to long words and exhausted idioms, like a cuttlefish spurting out ink. "
>
> George Orwell

I have personally been discovering and refining this Conscious Language™ Upgrade for 37 years. The system shared through this book has the potential to help you realize your Dreams in the twinkling of an eye. It just takes getting our eyes twinkling—i.e. be enthusiastic—*entheos,* God in you.

Knowing beforehand what each reactive tendency turns into on the action side of the equation helps you to transform any reaction—limitation—into your Highest Choice. Each of the first 11 domains described in chapters 5-15 can be transformed into its Divine Attribute *through* Conscious Language™.

Domains of Creativity, Outcome and Mastery

The Domain of Limitation and No-Choice upgrades
➡ The Domain of Opulent Choice.

The Domain of Non-Choice upgrades
➡ The Domain of True Choice.

The Domain of Ineffective Choice upgrades
➡ The Domain of Effective Choice.

The Domain of Absolutes and Grandiosities upgrades
➡ The Domain of Specificity.

The Domain of Conditional Choices upgrades
➡ The Domain of Clear Choice.

The Domain of the T's upgrades
➡ The Domain of Ownership.

The Domain of Cancellation upgrades
➡ The Domain of Confirmation.

The Domain of Process Without Outcome upgrades
➡ The Domain of Fulfilled Outcome.

The Domain of Co-Dependence upgrades
➡ The Domain of Co-Empowerment.

The Domain of Impersonal Disconnection upgrades
➡ The Domain of Connected, Personal Outcomes.

The Domain of Outcome, Almost upgrades
➡ The Domain of Specific Outcomes.

By a simple upgrade in Language, you can transform the eleven domains known collectively as the Domains of Self-Sabotage into the eleven Domains of Self-Success. Here's how to do it:

- To transform the Domain of Limitation and No Choice, change or remove the word *not* in its full and contracted forms (n't) and say what is or what you *do choose*. "I choose to make this easy!" "I choose to have ________."(Fill in the blank. Step into the **Domain of Opulent Choice!**)

- To upgrade the *Domain of Non-Choice* into the **Domain of True Choice**, start choosing what you desire instead of what you wish to avoid.

- To move through the *Domain of Ineffective Choice,* replace wimpy words with words of Commitment backed up by aligned feeling and move into the **Domain of Effective Choice!**

- To upgrade the *Domain of Absolutes and Grandiosities* remember to get real, specific and exact and move into the **Domain of Specificity!**

- To upgrade through the maze of the *Domain of Conditional Choice,* replace conditional statements—*in order to, so that*—with the word and and enter the **Domain of Clear Choice!**

- To connect through the separation of the *Domain of the T's,* make your communication personal and use words such as *our* and *my* and make contact with the **Domain of Ownership!**

- To reverse the *Domain of Cancellation,* cancel your use of conjunctions and contractions and use clear, specific language and move into the **Domain of Confirmation!**

- To resurrect the *Domain of Process without Outcome,* look beyond the activity—see the end from the beginning—and state your desired result into existence and step into the **Domain of Fulfilled Outcomes!**

- To heal the *Domain of Co-Dependence,* engage your own authority and inner integrity and step into the **Domain of Co-Empowerment!**

- To replace your self-imposed penance in the *Domain of Impersonal Disconnection,* upgrade your thinking and speaking to include who, what, where, when, and in what way, shape, and form you are included Consciously and enter the **Domain of Connected Personal Outcomes!**

- To blaze through the *Domain of Outcome, Almost,* add one or two more personal, aligned, specific steps to your thoughts or words and enter the **Domain of Outcome Fulfilled!**

THE POWER OF YOUR WORDS

Neville writes in his book *"Immortal Man[8]":*

> *"This whole manifested world goes to show us what use or misuse we have made of God's gift. And God's gift is your mind and your speech. It is not your outer speech, for we know how deceptive that is. God sees only the inside. Man sees the outer appearance and God sees the inner man.*
>
> *When you watch your inner conversations, you are actually watching your new nature. If you don't like it, change it and take of the old man and put on the new man and he will show you the salvation of God and then the whole thing will unfold within you."*

> When people talk, listen completely. Most people never listen.
> Ernest Hemingway

Your language is most fully potent when you realize your spoken words act as Decrees, sending forth their vibratory patterns into the Universe and magnetizing exactly what is spoken. The degree of your intensity, feeling and specificity as you speak determines how quickly your expression becomes your Reality. Your unseen Words become your seen experiences through the law of *"The word was made flesh."* When you change your language you change your vibration which potentially changes your Reality, depending on your level of feeling and specificity. Additional repetitions of your words in alignment with your beliefs increase the speed of manifestation.

By changing your language to emulate and vibrate with our Hearts' desires we manifest higher vibratory experiences in our lives. We can use our words to heal, to prosper, to flourish and to glorify our Creator and Creation. We can ensure that the prophecy fulfilled by our Word is one in which we are fully aligned.

---

[8] "The Immortal Man", DeVorss & Company, Publisher

> "It is the supreme art of the teacher to awaken joy in creative expression and knowledge."
> Albert Einstein

By waking up to our spoken words, we awaken our inner speech which is either unconscious—the old conversation, the outer self, the old man (woman)—or it is Conscious—our New Conversation, our Inner Self, our New Woman (Man).

> *"That ye put off concerning the former conversation the old man, which is corrupt according to the deceitful lusts; And be renewed in the spirit of your mind; And that ye put on the new man, which after God is created in righteousness and true holiness." Ephesians 4:22-24*

As our outer speech is practiced and we gain confidence and success, Miracles begin, like a metamorphosis and a New Man, a New Woman, a New Being Awakens. Our Hearts begin to speak. Our I can'ts turn into "I AM that I AM." Our Inner Speech becomes our Outer Pure Speech and great good is the result.

> *"Whoso offereth praise glorifieth me: and to him that ordereth his conversation aright will I shew the salvation of God." Psalm 50:23*

Practicing and lovingly encouraging each other, in our families, relationships, businesses, organizations, and Spiritual practices to speak and think in Conscious Language™ brings our Inner Speech up to the quality of life where our Victory lives.

> *22And Jesus answering smith unto them, Have faith in God.*
> *23For verily I say unto you, That whosoever shall say unto this mountain, Be thou removed and be thou cast into the sea; and shall not doubt in his heart, but shall believe that those things which he saith shall come to pass; he shall have whatsoever he saith.*
> *24Therefore I say unto you, What things so ever ye desire, when ye pray, believe that ye receive them and ye shall have them. Mark 11:22-24*

SAYING NO TO BABEL

Babel is a state of confusion. Babel is an agreement to be separate, disassociated and dispersed. When an individual or organization begins to upgrade to a new Conscious Human Operating System many memories or "files," programs, beliefs, agreements and histories may feel threatened because they will not function on the new program—belief system—Choice—Conscious Human Operating System.

Like old pesky viruses in our programs on our computers, Babel language patterns are a "stronghold" of limitation, separation, and confusion. Limitation's job is to maintain limitation—the way we created it—*limited*.

Healing the Babel Virus requires us to take dominion over our limitations with Love and resetting of our agreements, choices, beliefs by taking Conscious authority—authorship. Babel was delivered to humanity when humanity stepped off God's intended path.

Returning to God's Divine Plan requires:

- We know where God is—*within*
- We know what God's Name is—I AM—and
- We build our Temple—*within*—according to I AM that I AM's design.

Simple!
Imagine:

- Imagine what happens to feelings of lack when a person chooses to be abundant.
- Imagine how many hours, days and years the individual has proved and believed they were lacking something.
- Imagine how powerful the new choice must be to replace those deeply embedded memories of lack with abundance.
- Imagine how much Grace is already available to assist each one of us.

As you make new choices of being abundant there is a process of moving upscale. This awareness helps you know where you are and how far you have to go to fully install your new choice. The Scale of Emotional Harmonics which follows, is explained in detail in Mastery Sysrem's CD set titled "Transforming E-Motion into Motion."

E-Motion	Word Pattern	How to Upgrade
Unconscious	"I *don't Know.*" "I am *confused.*" "I am *unaware.*"	I can "*Choose to know.*"
Apathy	"I *can't.*" "It's *too hard.* "I *don't care.*"	"I *Can and I choose to make this easy, I do care.*"
Grief	"I have *always* felt this way." "I have *never* been."	Get personally specific.
Fear	"*What if.*"	Love. *Perfect Love casteth out all fear.*
Anger	"*They* did it to me." "*She* wouldn't let me." "*My parents* kept me from."	Take authority and authorship.
Pain	"It *hurts.*" "The *pain* is *too great.*"	Love owning your enthusiasm.
Enthusiasm	I AM, I Can.	Enjoy Yourself!

> "Stand upright, speak thy thoughts, declare The truth thou hast, that all may share; Be bold, proclaim it everywhere: They only live who dare."
>
> Voltaire

When you have the opportunity to witness the coaching process, you will experience how subtle the attempted "Babel reboot" is. It is very necessary for the new student of Conscious Language™ to be ultra-aware of what is being said, felt, and believed. Awareness insures continued success in changing old reactive patterns into new life giving patterns.

Be aware you have now placed Babel in the state of survival—hurt animals fight hard for their life. Instead of battling survival, enter Thrival. With Thrival comes the Consciousness of more than enough. Giving (Tithing) is a wonderful benefit of being aware of Thrival.

> "Nothing great was ever achieved without enthusiasm."
> Ralph Waldo Emerson

> *"Bring ye all the tithes into the storehouse, that there may be meat in mine house and prove me now herewith, saith the LORD of hosts, if I will not open you the windows of heaven and pour you out a blessing, that there shall not be room enough to receive it." Malachi 3:10*

Here are a few examples of how in one sentence Babel will show up while an individual is attempting to be successful.

Statement	Explanation
I *choose to have* all my bills paid on time this month *so I don't* have to *struggle* with bills anymore.	
I *choose to have* all my bills paid on time this month...	Conscious
...*so I don't* have to *struggle* with bills anymore	Babel rebooted and re-established again in the focus on don't and struggle.
UPGRADE: I choose to pay my bills on time this month and feel relaxed from here on about my finances.	

Statement	Explanation
I am committed to have my Divine Partner. I just *hope* that he *isn't like* all my other partners.	
I am committed to have my Divine Partner. I just *hope*...	*Hope* is a vague positive.
...that...	*That* equals separation (review Domain of the T's).
...he *isn't like* all my other partners	Whatever we put our attention upon is what happens, therefore Babel is rebooted and old partner qualities are attracted.
UPGRADE: I AM committed to being one with my Divine Partner who is—list new, positive qualities, like "Strong, Caring, etc..	

Statement	Explanation
My outcome is to be very fit, healthy, enthusiastic, and motivated in my new job, so *that* I can have time to get over the death of my father.	
My outcome is to be very fit, healthy, enthusiastic, and motivated in my new job, so *that...*	...*That,* review Domain of Conditional Choice.
so... I can have time to get over the death of my father.	Babel reboot, focus is left on what is not chosen or desired.
UPGRADE: My outcome is, I love being fit, healthy, enthusiastic, and motivated in my new job. I easily honor my father's passing and remember his love.	

Statement	Explanation
I love myself. I believe *that* I am *ready* to have my new life.	
I love myself. I believe *that...*	Babel reboot, that is from the Domain of the T's supporting separation.
...I am *ready...*	Process.
...to have my new life.	Vague.
UPGRADE: I Love myself and believe I AM my new life.	

Babel is a language system which, in the past, I affirm, was operating unconsciously. To operate in and with a new Conscious Human Operating System requires very dynamic and aware new language patterns. By gathering a team of like-minded and committed friends, family and coworkers to practice Conscious Language™, you will help your upgrade process immensely.

I have had the opportunity to share Conscious Language™ with many and have had the experience of being coached by more Light beings about my language than anyone I know. I AM grateful (great-full) for every suggestion I have received because each coaching helped me catch some limitation revealed through my language which I was not yet aware of. By lovingly coming together to help each other and ourselves speak Consciously, we resurrect our language, thoughts and our lives.

THE CONSCIOUSNESS OF CHOICE

Keep the following points in focus:

- **Coach yourself.** By coaching ourselves we are focused on self-correction and letting others learn by our example. By coaching others without invitation we can diminish the number of our friends rapidly. Coach only on invitation and with immense Love.

> "Few are those who see with their own eyes and feel with their own hearts."
> Albert Einstein

- **Have ownership.** By owning our feelings, choices and language we have the doorway to make our choice real, like owing "real" estate. Be in your picture. "I feel." "My love." Make sure you are connected to what you choose.

- **Speak from your Heart.** Speak with feeling from your Inner Self. Speak what is true to your Heart of Hearts and others will listen.

- **Be fully and completely present.** By speaking in the present, your "here and now," what you say happens "here and now." Babel, time and space are from the same self-sabotage format. Conscious Language™ is the Language of Now.

> "Realize deeply that the present moment is all you ever have."
> Eckhart Tolle

- **Be first person, personal, here and now.** Essential for Conscious Language™ is the speaker, thinker, feeler to be in his/her own experience. The difference is as simple as The money vs. My money; the love vs. My love/Our love, the goal vs. My goal.

- **Be honest, empowering, connected and unified.** Speak the truth with the focus of empowerment to connect and unify. Know the truth and it will set you free. State what is true, what you do feel and what is in your Heart, and your words will richly reward you.

- **Move from wrong/right and bad/good into Highest Choice.** Change: "I made a mistake" to "I choose to be successful this time." Change: "You are never on time" to "I empower you to be on time." If you think you did it wrong, your are focusing on wrong. Just make a new choice.

- **In sailing it is called tacking.** The percentage of the time a sailboat heading to Maui, Hawaii from San Francisco is directly on course is less than 1%, yet it can still arrive on the shore of the island of Maui by making many new choices—tacking.

- **Explore the first words that come to you, they have truth in them!** Possibly one of the biggest tools I have to share. By speaking your first thought, feeling, and words, you will discover what is going on inside. It may not be your full truth yet it will be more of your truth than you have been aware of so far. Ask yourself, "How do I feel right now?" Immediately answer with your first words. Now do this one hundred more times today and you will find out what is going on in your feelings.

- **Instead of moving away from something, move toward something.**
  - Getting rid of pain vs. bringing ease and comfort.
  - Quitting smoking vs. being a fresh air breather, less debt vs. more abundance.
  - It is easier staying on the road because our eyes are looking where we are going.

- Instead of stating what is not, state what is. Don't worry vs. Be happy. State what you do choose, feel, see, and love. God is a God of what is. The adversary is about what is not.

- **Leave on your screen of Consciousness your Highest Choice.** I have not felt well, so I choose health now. Please be on time. It is not OK with me if you show up late each time, so please be on time. Leave the positive on the screen so it can ring forever.

- **Be a committed listening to yourself and others.** Just being present and really listening to what a person is saying is healing for all involved. It does not mean listening with a response right on your tongue or criticism and internal dialogue about what they are saying. Just be present and listen to others and yourself. By listening through our stuff to our hearts, Miracles happen.

> "There are people who, instead of listening to what is being said to them, are already listening to what they are going to say themselves."
>
> Albert Guinon
>
> "The ear is the avenue to the heart."
>
> Voltaire

- **Use "Cancel, clear" and "In the past" to clean the slate.** If you have said something which does not serve you, clear it from your "screen" of consciousness and replace it with what you choose. Filling in the blanks with your positive is imperative to effectively move upscale.

- **Speak and think only that which you choose to have come into reality now and continuously.** This is the story of the entire book. What we put our attention upon, we become.

POINTS TO REMEMBER

- **Choice is always available.** Make your choice, even if there seems you don't have a choice and you will begin to lift the veil of the illusion. Does your Creator have choice? Maybe we do too. What is your choice?

"Thou shalt also decree a thing and it shall be established unto thee: and the light shall shine upon thy ways." Job 22:28

- **Specificity brings up feelings.** It takes feeling to bring healing. The more specific we are the more we feel and the more we are engaged with the physical reality of our being. Specificity is the doorway to manifestation.

- **Words spoken with feelings and specificity EQUAL manifestation.** Be specific in your choices while admitting what you feel and choosing specifically what will satisfy your Heart of Hearts. Right now, admit what you really choose in your life personally with exacting specificity and notice how

> "It is not enough to aim; you must hit. "
>
> Italian Proverb

your body responds. The more specific you are, the more you will begin to transform limitation into your highest choice.

- **Thoughts, words and emotions create our Reality.** I AM what I AM Conscious of Being. My thoughts, words and feelings shape my Consciousness which shapes my Reality. Do you choose to upgrade anything today?

"But the word is very nigh unto thee, in thy mouth and in thy heart, that thou mayest do it." Deuteronomy 30:14

MARGIN NOTES

Margin Notes is a system designed through many classes of transforming internal dialogue into being fully and completely present. Internal dialogue is any thought, feeling, body sensation, or memory that you are continually aware of that keeps you from being a committed listener or from being fully and completely present. If you experience internal dialogue, write these thoughts—internal dialogue—in the margin of your paper or on any piece of paper.

Writing internal dialogue is a way to free the "thought form" or "belief system" held in the subconscious mind. When these thoughts are written, the subconscious is acknowledged, quieted, and again we are able to easily concentrate.

Examples of Margin Notes:

- ✓ I'm cold.
- ✓ It's hot.
- ✓ It's going too fast.
- ✓ I'm afraid to try this in my life.
- ✓ I have to go to the bathroom.

- ✓ I don't understand.
- ✓ I'm tired.
- ✓ I'm hungry.
- ✓ I've got to make this work in my life.
- ✓ I can't wait to tell my husband about this.
- ✓ What if I don't have anybody in my life to speak with this way?
- ✓ How will I remember all of this?
- ✓ This probably won't work with so and so.

Frequently—maybe 99.999% of the time—internal dialogue is revealing the counterfeit of our new choices emerging from our subconscious mind.

Writing Margin Notes gives you the opportunity to make these new choices Consciously. By being Conscious of our internal dialogue we can upgrade any reactive pattern into our new choice directly, immediately and easily. Each reactive pattern has a corresponding strength within itself.

Examples:

If you are moving upscale with a change of Language or an increase of Love or Faith, the counterfeit may surface before the attribute arrives.

- *Unconscious* is *Conscious* returning.
- *Apathy* is *Caring* and *Ease* returning.
- *Grief* and *Sadness* is *Joy* returning.
- *Fear* is *Faith* returning.
  - If you notice fear rising in your gut, know it is speeding you up to the frequency of confidence, faith, security, courage, and assuredness.
- *Anger* is *Forgiveness, Action and Authority* returning.

- If anger arises, know you are to the point where blaming others for your situations is about to be corrected. Love the anger and forgive and take your own authorship back and start creating your own life.
- *Pain* is *intuition* and *Enthusiastic Love* returning.

Awareness of what is returning gives great power to your Inner Self. Transform any reaction into your Loving Action.

MORE ON FIRST WORDS

Give yourself a wonderful and fast way to know what you choose by admitting what your subconscious self has for you. First Words is a very effective way to find out what is on your subconscious playing field. By stating your First Words about a choice or a situation you will know what was right at the top of the list to be dealt with from your emotional realm. First words can be used to quickly know what you choose. Usually our First Word response is accurate or holds important information to our choice process. If you do not like your First Words, try your second words, third and so on. Let your Inner Truths come out and play.

Story: I was sharing the event Mastery, Embodying Conscious Language™ and we were doing a process of alignment. One of the participants was having a challenge finding out what he felt about something. I asked him to say the first thing that came to him and after saying "first words" 4 or 5 times to him he blurts out "Chicken soup!" My first reaction was, "It isn't going to work this time." I waited and with a bit more coaching he uncovered a memory of his mother and her chicken soup and how much he misses her and tears flowed from most folks in class. I have witnessed thousands of First Word responses bringing individuals to a powerful understanding. For me too!

What is your goal in your life right now, first words? Be specific, make a full sentence, be first person, personal. Let yourself have it now!

To be fulfilled, happy, joyful, and enthusiastic is what most people desire and is the promise of life. Knowing and experiencing we have a Heart center and listening to it can change our lives and worlds.

Many times in working with individuals, we discover doubt that we really have a choice. Settling and making do is more the flavor of deep levels of limitations, struggle and lack. When we hear "make a choice" or "make our highest choice," this can be threatening and way outside our comfort zone.

We have been the ones to keep ourselves limited. Initiating the choosing process by being aware we have a choice and by reestablishing trust in life's ability to respond to our choices; we wake up to the question "What am I going to choose? What will satisfy me?"

> **Most of the choices of preconscious Language™ and preconscious Choice are choosing only what seems possible and reasonable.**

Highest choice, on the other hand, is a new idea. You mean to say I actually can choose my highest choice. Yes, I say, as long as it is in your Heart of Hearts and not just I want a whole bunch more stuff because it is cool to have more of this and that. Unless we choose our highest choice, our Hearts desire, we will self-sabotage anyway.

> **Anything less than our highest choice is serving limitation, fear and lack and can only bring something which keeps us settling instead of thriving.**

By committing to your highest choice, you will discover many required upgrades available to you. Using the tools of Conscious Language™ and Conscious Choice will help you live and thrive in your Conscious Life.

Making new choices which are Conscious and creative require some attention to detail and an awareness of your Heart's Desire.

As you initiate your new choices, review the following list of qualities which help make your new Human Operating System, Conscious and beneficial for you.

CHECK LIST FOR ATTAINED OUTCOMES

Ask yourself, is it...

- ✓ Specific
- ✓ Clear
- ✓ Definite
- ✓ Positive

Ask yourself, does it...

- ✓ Serve your highest good
- ✓ Create WIN/WIN
- ✓ Benefit all involved
- ✓ Satisfy you personally

Are you:

- ✓ Aligned with your desire?
- ✓ Claiming your desire?
- ✓ Receiving your desire?
- ✓ Satisfied with your fulfilled desire?

Strategy Specifics Checklist

- ✓ how much?
- ✓ how many?
- ✓ how often?
- ✓ with whom?
- ✓ when?
- ✓ where?

- ✓ in what way(s)?
- ✓ in what situations?
- ✓ having what?
- ✓ feeling what?
- ✓ hearing, seeing, being what?

DECREE A THING…

Words are the creative force of Spirit. If we say something less than our ideal, having quick corrections to keep us on track is powerful.

To Neutralize a statement, yours or someone else's say silently:

- Cancel clear!
- In the past!
- That has no power!

To Neutralize and requalify a statement:

- Cancel Clear and now I choose!
- In the past and now I …
- That has no power and I give power to …

Examples:

- "You are stupid."—"Cancel clear, I AM brilliant."
- "I feel sick"—"in the past and now I choose to feel great!"
- "We are going to have a wreck"—"Cancel clear, that has no power, I AM God driving this car and we are always safe and secure."

In every upgrade:

- Speak with authority and conviction.
- Take charge of the energy and make your statement as you choose according to your Inner Truth.

- Make every limited statement bow before your I AM and Decree what you choose until you get it.
- Say your Decree audibly, say it silently with all the feeling you have.
- Remember constantly, "Decree a thing and it shall be established unto you."
- Keep present in your Consciousness, I AM That I AM.
- Remember: In the Beginning of every new manifestation is the Word.

Our ability to think and say Words is a gift from our Creator. Use them wisely, powerfully, lovingly and to Bless all Life and manifest reality.

IN SUMMARY:

- *Think and feel before you speak.*
- *Experience the trajectory of your conversation and find out if your words actually take you to the place where you choose to be.*
- *Silence can be golden.*
- *Words are powerful.*
- *The full power of our language is released when we speak what we choose to have come into reality with feeling and alignment.*
- *Pure Speech already resides in our Heart of Hearts.*
- *Let your Heart speak, find your Heartware and become your "Heartdrive".*

WORDS TO UPGRADE

I want	I can't	Kind of
I would	At least	Didn't you
I need	I don't know	Almost
I could	Won't it	If/then
I should	It's hard	Probably
I might	Try	When/then
I hope	Doesn't it	Perhaps
I wish	Can't you	I feel that
I must	I hate	Decide
In order to	It bugs me	I feel you did
I have to	But	Always/Never
So that	Wouldn't you	Shouldn't you
I've got to	However	Isn't it
If all else fails	Can't you	

EXAMPLES OF BABEL UPGRADED TO CONSCIOUS LANGUAGE™

(These are only suggestions)

Statement ➡	**Upgrades to**
It's *hard* to imagine.	I Imagine with ease.
Don't forget to...	Please remember to...
You don't have to be a genius to figure this out.	This is easy.
Don't worry about it.	Be confident about it.
You can't go wrong.	You will do well.
You *needn't* take that into consideration.	All you require taking into account is.
That *couldn't* be further from the truth.	The truth is...
I remember the lessons that were *the most painfully* learned.	I learn through all my experiences.
Shouldn't you consider this?	Please consider this.
That's *not a bad* idea.	That is a good idea.
I foresee *no problems.*	I foresee ease.
Don't make me unhappy.	Please support our happiness.
Incredible. (Means without credibility.)	Wonderful.
I *won't* make any difference.	I will be present to support...
This'll knock them dead.	This will inspire them.
Obviously.	It is clear to me.
I *don't* care.	What I care about is...

Statement ➡	Upgrades to
It *doesn't* make any difference.	What is important to me is…
You'll *never believe* this.	This may surprise you.
You *lost me* on that one.	Please say that again.
That really *irks* me.	What I choose about this is…
I can *never figure* out...	I choose to easily figure this out.
I *can't* wait.	I choose to be patient and calm.
You *can't count* on anyone but yourself.	I can count on myself and I choose to have friends who I can rely upon.
I have to do it myself.	I will do it myself. Will you help me do this?
I always end up having to do it myself.	In the past I have ended up doing this myself, will you give me a hand this time?
What do you *want*?	How can I help you? What is your pleasure? Have you made your choice?
No problem.	My pleasure. You are welcome.
It looks like *I won't be able to* come.	I may be staying home.
I think I understand.	I choose to understand so let us review it again until I fully understand.
That went *over my head.*	Please repeat that again. I choose to understand.
Let me run this by you.	I have an idea I choose to share.
Can I bounce my idea off you?	May I share my idea with you? What is your take on my idea?
Can I pick your brain?	Will you share your ideas on…?
I don't mean to bother you.	Is this a good time to share about…?

Statement ➡	Upgrades to
Can't you help?	Can you please help me…?
Isn't it time to go?	Is it time to go?
Wouldn't it be nice?	Is this nice?
It blows my mind.	It expands my consciousness greatly.
That *kills* me.	That is awesome to me.
It's to *die* for.	It's to live for.
Killer.	Awesome. Wonderful. Dude, how cool.
Absolutely.	"Absolutely Yes" or "Absolutely No."
Don't be home *late.*	Be home on time.
Don't forget to vote.	Remember to vote.
I hope *I didn't bother* you.	Did I interrupt? Is this a good time?
Don't make a mistake.	Focus on getting it the first time.
Don't act stupid.	Remember your brilliance.
Don't tell anyone.	Please keep this between us. It is private.
He is *not doing* well.	Let us imagine him doing well.
I am afraid things are going downhill.	I choose to feel confident things are going well. Will you affirm with me things are going well?
Stop doing that.	Start doing this. Instead of doing that, please do this.
"My bad." (slang).	I apologize. Oops!

Statement ➡	Upgrades to
I *forgot* what I was doing.	I choose to remember what I was doing.
I am afraid I will fail.	I choose to be successful. I AM successful now and continuously. I Decree my success. God in me is my success.
I hope *they don't screw* this up.	I empower them to do a great job and be victorious.
This *hurts too much.*	I feel great pain and I choose to transform it into love and strength.
Please *don't* take this *wrong.*	Please take this with love and understanding.
This conversation *sucks.*	Let us talk about something more pleasant.
I *don't* trust you.	I choose to trust you and what I require to trust you is…
I have *worried* about this all my life.	I have felt worry about this a lot in the past and now I choose to feel confident.
I *don't* believe that.	What I believe is….
You make me sad.	I experience sadness when you do that. I choose to feel joy about…
You *always* see the *worst* in me	Please see the best in me.
I *don't like* what I see.	I imagine seeing…
I *never* get ahead.	I choose to get ahead. I choose to have ___ dollars in my account by ____.
You always watch TV.	Can we do something different tonight? Will you please go for a walk with me?
What if I *can't* afford it?	My "I AM" can easily afford it. I choose to easily afford it. I AM affording it with ease.
I am *looking for* the answer.	I AM finding the answer.
I am *looking for* my Divine Partner.	I choose to have my Divine Partner now. I AM one with my Divine Partner now and forever.

Statement ➡	Upgrades to
Don't fall.	Be careful. Hold on.
Don't get hurt.	Be safe.
I *almost feel* secure.	I claim my security.
I *can't afford* a ticket.	I will increase my cash flow to afford a ticket.
I have *spent* lots of time on…	I have invested lots of time on…
I *spent* a lot on you.	I invested a lot in you.
I *spent* my whole life.	I invested much of my energy on…
I am *tired.*	I choose to be energized.
I have *got to* go to sleep.	I choose to rest now.
I *never have* enough energy.	I claim my Divine Energy now.
It *blows* me away.	I AM inspired. I AM awed.
I *feel* like…	I feel-what feeling? (*I feel like* are the three words of Co-Dependence.)
I *feel* that… (*That is not a feeling.*)	I feel what?
I *love to spoil* her rotten.	I love to bless her greatly.
What the *hell?*	What the Heaven?
Money is the root of all *evil.*	I bless all money that comes into my hands and use and command it bless all life. Money is only Energy, which I have plenty of…
Filthy rich.	Blessed abundantly.
It is my *fault.*	It is my responsibility.
I am *part of* the team.	I AM on the team.
I *decide.*	I choose. The word "decide" means "of death." Insecticide, suicide, homicide, genocide.

Statement ➡	Upgrades to
My *decision* is.	My choice is.
The possibilities are *limitless.*	The possibilities are ever expanding.- (Limitless is less limited)
The possibilities are *endless.*	The possibilities go on forever.
He won *in spite of* himself.	He won and turned his weaknesses into his strengths.-(In "spite" of is in "hate" of.)
The course was *unerring.*	The course was true.
I *am not* feeling well.	I AM choosing health.
Damn it!	Bless it!
I *feel like* you should…	I empower you to…
I *can't* go.	I AM staying here.
The *truth is* hard to come by.	The truth takes determination.
Quit being nervous.	Relax.
Stop worrying.	Trust.
Don't get confused.	Be clear.
Don't worry about it.	Have faith. Trust!
We are *there.*	We are here.
We did it *all* wrong.	We could have done it differently. We will do it right this time.
Time *will heal* this.	It is—I AM—healed now.
Quit being *messy.*	Start being neat.
God *was* there for me.	God is here for me.

Statement ➡	Upgrades to
I *need* your help.	I require help, will you help me?
I *can't* handle this.	I choose to easily handle this.
What is your problem?	How can I support you?
I *have a bad* back.	I AM healing my back; will you lift this for me?
I *have arthritis.*	I AM choosing comfort and flexibility in my joints.
My adrenals *are shot.*	I AM restoring peacefulness and calmness and resilience in my life.
I *forgot* my keys.	I just remembered my keys and will go get them.
I am *weak.*	I AM strong. I choose strength. God in me is strong there for I AM strong.
I feel *confused.*	I feel—state what you do feel in your emotions or body.
The market is *slow.*	I find success in whatever the market appears to be doing.
I give you 6 months to live.	Unless we change something, I have seen people live 6 more months. Miracles happen.
This is *incurable.*	I have yet to see this condition cure. We will have to go to a Higher Authority to find a cure.
Your heart *is in bad* shape.	Your heart requires lots of support to heal.

SECTION D

APPENDICES

APPENDIX 1

REWRITE EMPOWERMENT EXERCISE

Rewrite These Phrases Using Your Version Of Conscious Language™

I have included the following phrases gleaned from Corporate and Government Agency Trainings. Please take a separate piece of paper and write your upgrades using Conscious Language™ that feels good to you. Take each phrase or statement as if you had just said it or thought it YOURSELF. After doing this exercise, check your ideas with other possibilities given in Appendix 3.

This is a very helpful exercise. Most people find it supportive to becoming automatic Conscious.

1. I *can't* understand.
2. I'm *never* on time.
3. I choose *not* to go.
4. I *want* you to help me.
5. *If* I can afford it.
6. I have a *hard* time.
7. They *don't* understand.
8. This is going to be *difficult.*
9. *What* if they *won't* help me?
10. They always put me…
11. My boss *won't* listen to me.
12. This is the *only* job available.
13. I *have* to get this done.
14. Time is running out.
15. I am overweight.
16. I am working on it.
17. I am choosing to lose weight.
18. My parents *never allowed* me to.
19. I always have to work hard.
20. My *problem* is.
21. You *never* do it right.
22. You are *not* cut out for that job.
23. We are really *mismatched.*
24. I *hope* you understand the situation.
25. I *don't* think I'm treated fairly.
26. I *can't* change things here.
27. I'm *not* recognized.
28. There's *too much* work.
29. We *need* more people.
30. There are *unhappy* people here.
31. I *don't feel* free to enjoy my work.
32. They have ways to *get you.*
33. They don't trust us.
34. *People won't say* what they really think.
35. *We don't* have enough information.
36. She complains too much.
37. I feel *like* I'm *stifled.*
38. Management gives us *no support.*

39. They are controlling.
40. *Nobody wants* to take responsibility.
41. They blame us.
42. *It won't* heal itself.
43. They *don't* know what's happening.
44. They don't care.
45. *There's no* resolution.
46. It's *difficult* to advance.
47. *There's no respect* for confidentiality.
48. I don't want to feel left out.
49. I *don't know* why *things* happen.
50. I *worry* about what I say.
51. They *can't get away* with it.
52. They *should* apologize.
53. I *can't* do it anymore.
54. It's *hard* to stay focused on positive.
55. It's totally unfair.
56. I *can't* believe it.
57. *There's no* equality.
58. You make me angry.
59. It *makes me* sad.
60. It's *always* been like this.
61. I *have to* do what they *want.*
62. You just don't get it.

APPENDIX 2

UPGRADING YOUR HUMAN OPERATING SYSTEM

Here are some examples of rewriting the limiting language on pages 165 to 167 using Conscious Language™ and Language of Mastery. Please remember, these are only suggested rewrites.

LIMITING LANGUAGE ➡ UPGRADES TO	
I can't understand.	I choose to understand. I empower myself to understand. I give myself permission to understand. I do what it takes to understand.
I'm never on time.	In the past I was late and now I choose to be on time. I AM on time. I AM committed to being on time with ease. I keep my own time schedule. I enjoy being successful in being on time.
I choose not to go.	I AM staying here. I choose to stay here.
I want you to help me.	Please help me. Will you help me? I require your help, are you available?
If I can afford it.	I choose to be able to afford it. I can afford it. If I choose to invest my resources in this way.

LIMITING LANGUAGE ➡ UPGRADES TO	
I have a hard time.	In the past, I had a hard time. Now I choose to make it fun and easy. I empower myself to make this easy.
They don't	To understand this, they require extra support.
understand.	They say they do not understand. I empower them to understand. In the past they had a challenge understanding. I will do what I can to help them understand.
This is going to be difficult.	I empower this to be easy. I will remain focused until my project is complete to my satisfaction.
What if they won't help me?	I always have what I require. I empower them to help me. I always attract the support I require. If it is not them (state names specifically), I will easily find someone else.
They always put me...	I have created being put... and now I create...They always put me ______, in the past and now my choice is...
My boss won't listen to me.	In the past I have believed and proved, my boss did not listen to me. I now empower my boss to listen to me. I choose to have a boss who is my partner. It's up to me to realize I AM worthy of being listened to by my boss. By partnering with my boss, I can insure my boss listens to me.
This is the only job available.	There are many jobs available to me. This job is available. I empower myself to find a great job.
I have to get this done.	I AM getting my job done. I AM completing by job with ease. I AM enjoying doing this job in a timely manner.
Time is running out.	It's important to me to complete this in the time assigned. I AM completing my task in the available time.
I am overweight.	I weigh ________lbs. and I choose to weigh ________lbs. I choose to wear a size ______shirt, dress, slacks. I choose to be comfortable in my body.
I am working on it.	I AM completing it. I AM doing it.

LIMITING LANGUAGE ➡ UPGRADES TO	
My parents never allowed me to.	My parents said I was not allowed to and I believed them. Now my choice is...I created not being allowed to by my parents and my new choice is...
I always have to work hard.	I have believed, in the past, I had to work hard and now I choose to work smart. I love to work effectively. I empower myself to work smart, with ease.
My problem is;	My opportunity is. My challenge is. This is my situation. I AM claiming victory in...
You never do it right.	Please focus and do it right. It's important to me to have this done right.
You are not cut out for that job.	You are better suited for a different job. You are skilled in other areas. Your skills in this area require upgrading.
We are really mismatched.	We do things different from each other. Let's see in we can be complements of each other's approach. I approach things in a different way than you do.
I hope you understand the situation.	Do you understand the situation? Please understand the situation.
I don't think I'm treated fairly.	I believe I have been treated unfairly. Please treat me fairly. It's up to me to empower myself to be treated fairly.
I can't change things here.	In the past, I believed I could not change things. Now I choose to change things. I empower things to change into I can change things here.
I'm not recognized.	I choose to be recognized—by, how, in what way, when. I empower myself to be recognized...I recognize myself for...
There's too much work.	I have much work to accomplish. I choose to do it with ease and effectiveness. I choose to accomplish my task with ease. To do so, I request help from... I do my appointed tasks with ease. I remain focused on completing my work on time.
We need more people.	We require ___ number of people. I choose to have ___ people.

LIMITING LANGUAGE →	UPGRADES TO
There are unhappy people here.	Some people here could be much happier. I empower people here to be happy.
I don't feel free to enjoy my work.	I choose to feel free to enjoy my work. To enjoy my work, I require...I feel anger about being restricted at work. I empower myself to forgive ______ and create my enjoyment of my work with ease.
They have ways to get you.	Cancel clear. I choose to be supported and appreciated for my contribution by ____.
They don't trust us.	In the past I—believed, felt, thought, feared, proved—that they do not trust us and now I choose to be trusted. I empower them to trust us. I AM trustworthy and they—be specific—know it. I will do _____ to insure they realize I AM trustworthy.
People won't say what they really think.	In the past, I found people did not say what they really think. I now empower myself and people—be specific—to say what we really think.
We don't have enough information.	I AM committed to being effective. Please give me more information about...I choose to understand and therefore I require more information. We can get enough information by asking ______ .
She complains too much.	I empower her—be specific—to focus on solutions.
Issues are blown out of proportion.	Let us bring these issues into perspective.
I feel like I'm stifled.	I feel stifled and I choose to feel expanded and creative.
Management gives us no support.	I empower management to support us by...In the past, I experienced lack of support from management. I now choose to experience management supporting us fully.
They are controlling.	I choose to experience partnership with them—be specific—in guiding our project.

LIMITING LANGUAGE ➡ UPGRADES TO	
Nobody wants to take responsibility.	Let us develop effective levels of responsibility. I empower our team to be responsible. I AM responsible for my task as well as the project as a whole. I empower my team members to find their own enthusiastic responsibility.
They blame us.	In the past, I feared they blame us. Now I choose to be honored by them and work as a team.
It won't heal itself.	I imagine this—be specific—being healed into _____.
They don't know what's happening.	It appears they don't know what is happening, so I will educate them. I will share with them what is happening.
They don't care.	I imagine them caring. I empower them to enjoy caring. I choose to be in an environment that cares. I will bring my concerns to their attention.
There's no resolution.	I choose to know how to resolve this situation with win/win for all involved. I empower us to come to resolution with ease.
It's difficult to advance.	I choose to meet the challenge of advancing with ease. Even in this challenging environment, I empower myself to advance successfully. I commit to advance to _______ (position) by _______ (date).
There's no respect for confidentiality.	I respect confidentiality. I empower our team to have agreements about confidentiality.
I don't want to feel left out.	I choose to feel included. I don't know why things happen. I AM interested in knowing why things—be specific—happen. I choose to know why _______ happened. I empower ________ to happen.
I worry about what I say.	I choose to be confident about what I say. I say what I mean with ease. I speak from my heart and I AM understood. I communicate confidently.
They can't get away with it.	I empower them to be responsible for their actions.

LIMITING LANGUAGE ➡ UPGRADES TO	
They should apologize.	I imagine them apologizing. I empower them to take responsibility and apologize. ________ deserves an apology from them.
I can't do it anymore.	I choose to change what I do into ______. I can do it with ease. I AM complete with struggle and now I choose ease. To be able to do this with ease, I require...
It's hard to stay focused on positive.	I AM positive. I remain positive with ease. I choose to stay focused on positive with ease. I AM committed to remaining positive.
It's totally unfair.	I empower fairness in ____.To make this fair, I choose ____.
I can't believe it.	I can believe it. What I believe is... In the past I could not believe it and now I...
There's no equality.	I choose equality in...
You make me angry.	I experience anger when you...
It makes me sad.	I feel sad when _____ happens. I choose to feel joy about...
It's always been like this.	For _____ length of time is has been like this. I now choose...
I have to do what they want.	I do this because I choose to. I AM keeping my agreements by doing...
You just don't get it.	I choose to help you get it. I commit to having you get it. I empower you to get it.
You can get it.	Now that you get it how do you feel?

APPENDIX 3

UPGRADING IN REAL TIME

The keys in successfully applying the tools found in *Conscious Language!*

Many times I have discovered myself "trying to say it right" and ultimately missed the point of honoring where I currently found myself. I have discovered making a new choice requires knowing the "truth which sets me free" to make a new choice. Using these language tools has improved my effectiveness in sharing these concepts with my students and friends.

In a classroom, it is very easy coaching participants by asking questions and using their answer, to offer new options in language which guide them upscale into their manifest heart's desire. Writing offers its own challenges and rewards in helping you, the reader, fully understand the principles of upgrading your life through your language awareness. *I choose to make this easy for both of us!*

Any word pattern you discover that is less than your highest choice is upgradeable. It is very important to find a real upgrade, not just a cover over or vague attempt.

Since the 80's, I have noticed in the communities of graduates of Conscious Language™—many whom have become friends—some are successful and thriving using CL tools and others are in a loop of not manifesting their success. Many of them use the phrase "I choose… happiness, love, abundance or some other state or situation." I find, in listening to these friends, a common error in speaking: While some are manifesting, creating, and enjoying their new lives, others, seemingly using the "right" words, are still not having their dreams manifest.

I will explain. To choose is to move toward something. It does not mean the desired outcome is attained. To be vague gives only enough information to create frustration, stress and disease to all involved.

Example: "I don't know." Vague upgrade: "I choose to know." I choose to know is only a shift toward knowing. The next step is to take action and *actually CHOOSE TO KNOW* and find out. Either let your inner self instruct you, ask someone who knows, go online and do research, pray or do something which lets your inner being know you mean what you say.

> **"I choose to know" is only "I don't know" using different words if you do not immediately take the next steps of finding out.**

Example:

1. **Old Pattern:** "I don't understand how to forgive."

2. **Vague pattern attempt:** "I choose to understand how to forgive."

3. **New Pattern:** "I choose to understand how to forgive my brother for breaking my arrow and for disrespecting me by not taking care of my things.
   - I choose—choose is process only and does not indicate a new state, just a choice to have a new state.
   - to understand how to forgive my brother for breaking my arrow and for disrespecting me by not taking care my things—here greater specificity is revealed.

4. **Upgrade Pattern:** "I forgive my brother for not respecting me and my things and breaking my arrow. I empower my brother to respect me and my belongings. I see my brother respecting himself and our family."

The more specific we are, the greater the amount of information is engaged and the greater the amount of feeling is experienced. Feeling is the beginning of healing. No feeling, no healing. Faith is feeling. If we go at things mentally, conceptually, we will only have vague manifestations. When we are courageous enough to speak—even to ourselves—with specificity, miracles happen. Our words become flesh.

> *"Faith is the substance of things hoped for, the evidence of things unseen."*

To make a Decree without being in the picture extends the level of separation.

Question: "What is your outcome?"
Answer: "Happiness." Here the person defines a state free from their own connection to it.

New A. 1. "I am happy." Now it is personal, yet vague.
New A. 2. "I AM *happy* with my new job." In this case, things are beginning to happen for this person. They are in the picture—*I AM*—and have identified a new state of being-happy—with specificity—with my new job.

It is essential for the individual to keep being more and more specific until the old self gives way to the new self, the new state, the new desired outcome. In our classes, I call this speaking an aligned statement.

"Decree a thing and it shall be established unto you." To Decree is to speak with authority, feeling, and specificity. In the case of the above example. "I AM happy with my new job" the individual may not shake their old belief enough due to some pattern, feeling, memory, or "reality" which is still holding on and not yet fully replaced.

The idea here is to *fully* transform any old pattern into your new pattern. I love calling this "REPLACEMENT THERAPY" because it actually replaces—transforms, transmutes—one set of energies with a new set. Then we are not getting rid of a pattern, we are actually re-nouncing—re-naming—one pattern into another.

Any state, feeling, situation, or condition is only a set of agreements, definitions and rates of vibrations. It was all created by the WORD, therefore we can RE-WORD it. Again, the key is to reword it with feeling, specificity, in first person, personal Consciousness. "I AM happy with my new job" may only transform the old state when enough specificity—the factor which engages our feeling—is present.

"I AM happy with my new job, which:

- ✓ pays me $200,000 a year.
- ✓ gives me every weekend off for myself and my family.
- ✓ provides me great health benefits—and then state what "great" means.
- ✓ is a service to humanity.
- ✓ provides me ownership potential.
- ✓ has a paid training program for advancement."

In the Outcome Facilitation™ System I employ in every class, I ask the individual, "What is the outcome of …" and find out if her new job is the real answer, with enough specificity to invoke a new state of being. Her answer might be, "The outcome of that is I trust God again." Or "I relax in my family's love." When she answers with something which demonstrates a new state of being, then her language upgrade has become her new current reality, her new state of being. Her Decree has been established within her being and Consciousness and will out-picture into her reality. Her word has become flesh.

Speak with feeling, specificity, in first-person, personally, identifying your outcome as here and now.

In "REPLACEMENT THERAPY" each aspect or word of the old pattern is to be upgraded into your desired new pattern. Even a word left out can create self-sabotage.

Example:

1. **Old Pattern:** "I hate being last in school and having everyone look at me with distain."
2. **Attempted new pattern:** " I love being first in school." Here the entire energy package has not been fully addressed.
3. **New Pattern:** " I love being first in school and I enjoy being congratulated."
   - "Everyone looking at me with distain" has now been addressed and most likely even if this person was first in school, the belief, agreement, and limited Decree would not be upgraded.
4. **Upgrade Pattern:** " I love being first in school and I enjoy being congratulated by my peers, teachers, and administrators, including (names of peers, teachers and administrators). I AM congratulated for—state the exact things being congratulated." The upgrade occurs in the specifity. Remember, the more specific we are, the more instantaneous the manifestation.

Consciousness returns Consciously. The unseen forces of life—I believe they are Angelic—operate on our words alone. The more specific we are, the more information our subconscious mind and our Divine Support Team have to go on to bring about out Decree.

I have witnessed many individuals very accurately describe their limited states, with exacting specificity and only vaguely come up with a notion of some type of wishy-washy idea of what to turn it into. I have discovered *the basis of the vagueness is fear.* Any goal originated from fear will not be rewarded from our Great Inner Being.

Serving faith makes the unseen become seen. Faith is our Activator, our Connector, our Manifestor. Since faith is a feeling and specificity brings up feeling, specificity and faith work together.

> "I've come to believe that each of us has a personal calling that's as unique as a fingerprint and that the best way to succeed is to discover what you love and then find a way to offer it to others in the form of service, working hard and also allowing the energy of the universe to lead you."
> Oprah Winfrey, *O Magazine*, Sept. 2002

Belief shapes our Reality. Thoughts integrated with feelings form our Beliefs which in turn shape our Reality.

Our Reality is what we make up and prove to be true. Reality, for us, is what we believe to be true. Beliefs—thoughts, shaped with language and feelings—actualize themselves into existence because our Inner world becomes our outer world. As a man (woman) thinketh in his (her) heart, so is he (she). Is essential for those choosing to Consciously Co-Create their lives to understand their role in manifestation.

Our Consciousness—awareness—directly attracts/creates/magnetizes/coalesces our outer reality.

Beliefs are deeper and more powerful than I ever realized in my early years of awakening. Beliefs actually define our existence. Language ultimately defines belief. Belief is changed through linguistic determination.

> "There is only one admirable form of the imagination: the imagination that is so intense that it creates a new reality, that it makes things happen."
>
> Sean O'Faolain

Example:

1. Say out loud: *"I want* Love."
2. Say out loud: *"I have* Love."
1. Say out loud: *"I want* Love."
2. Say out loud: *"I have* Love."
1. Say out loud: *"I want* Love."
2. Say out loud: *"I have* Love."

1. Say out loud: *"I want* Love."
2. Say out loud: *"I AM* Love."
1. Say out loud: *"I want* Love."
2. Say out loud: *"I AM* Love."
1. Say out loud: *"I want* Love."
2. Say out loud: *"I AM* Love."

1. Say out loud: *"I want* Love."
2. Say out loud: *"I love* Love."
1. Say out loud: *"I want* Love."
2. Say out loud: *"I love* Love."
1. Say out loud: *"I want* Love."
2. Say out loud: *"I love* Love."

How do you *feel* with the second statement in each series? Do you *feel* different with having, being, and loving Love? If so, the feeling change is the beginning of your Belief change. I describe this positive change as Upgrading your Belief. Beliefs are changeable, upgradeable, transformable, transmutable. *Belief is up to us* as Co-Creators.

"A man who offendeth not in word is able to bridle the whole body" describes a state of conscious speaking where the Lord's Name—I AM—is not being made in vain. By offending not in word, the Self, I AM that I AM, is honored, revered, believed in and controls the whole body. The tongue in the rudder of our ship because is shapes belief which shapes our Reality. Language shapes reality.

I have discovered the Scriptures are descriptions of states of Consciousness. *"I will return to you a pure Speech"*—also translated "pure language" Zephaniah 3:9—refers to a state of Consciousness, not some time in some distant future. The individual remembers who they are—I AM that I AM—and when they are—NOW! Babble is replaced with Pure Speech, where in Consciousness we remember (re-unify) we are what we Decree; we are what we are Conscious of Being, what we Desire (of the Stars) is already here and now as God is Here and Now.

Pure Speech is right here, in you and me, right now! "I AM" is right here, right now! "I have" is right here, right now! Yes, the outer world may show a different appearance.

It requires Faith, Trust, Confidence, Security, and Courage to observe your perceived limited state and announce a new state within yourself with Faith birthing your new Reality.

- If you could, would you be full of Faith, Trust, Confidence, Security, and Courage?
- If you could, would you be a Realized Being of the most High Living God and Co-Create according to your Heart of Heart's Desires blessing all life, including yourself?
- If you were one with God, would you have come up with a Divine Plan awaiting discovery by your created son or daughter?
- If you were God, would you have created an outer Savior or an Inner Savior residing in the Heart of your Creation?

- Would you have created a way back home through the illusion by using fear, doubt, and separation or Love, Faith, and Union?

As one being—Adam—fell from Grace and created separation another Being arose and remembered Union. *"I AM the resurrection and the life"* reportedly were the words Christ used to change His belief and ultimately Ascend to the Father. He said, *"These things that I do, ye shall do also, yea even greater things shall ye do, because I go unto my Father."*

What do you Choose to Create in your Life Right Now?

What happens when we repeat the Decree, "I AM the resurrection and the life" until we feel—Believe—in every cell in our body?

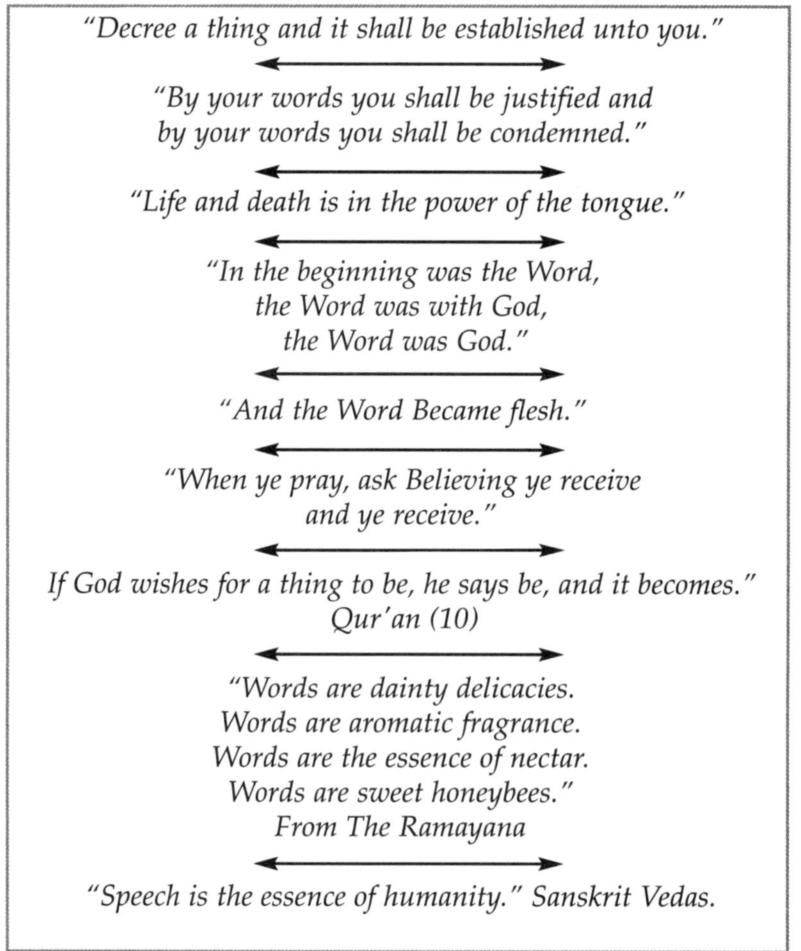

"Decree a thing and it shall be established unto you."

"By your words you shall be justified and by your words you shall be condemned."

"Life and death is in the power of the tongue."

"In the beginning was the Word,
the Word was with God,
the Word was God."

"And the Word Became flesh."

"When ye pray, ask Believing ye receive and ye receive."

If God wishes for a thing to be, he says be, and it becomes."
Qur'an (10)

"Words are dainty delicacies.
Words are aromatic fragrance.
Words are the essence of nectar.
Words are sweet honeybees."
From The Ramayana

"Speech is the essence of humanity." Sanskrit Vedas.

Upgrades to:

The God.	*Upgrades to*	My God!
The body.	*Upgrades to*	My Body!
The Planet.	*Upgrades to*	Our Planet!

Be the miracle you desire. Acquire what your require!

Let your Beliefs be the Choir singing
into manifestation your acquired requirements.

I AM
I CAM
I WILL
I CHOOSE
I HAVE
I LOVE
I CREATE
I ENJOY

I AM Heaven on Earth now and continuously!

I AM the resurrection and the Life of
all Humanity in perfect Divine Order!

I AM God's Divine Plan fulfilled God's Way!

APPENDIX 4

REVIEWING SELECTED SCRIPTURES FOR LANGUAGE AWARENESS

Genesis 1:

1 In the beginning God created the heaven and the earth. 3 And God said, Let there be light: and there was light.

Genesis 11:

1 And the whole earth was of one language and of one speech. 4 And they said, Go to, let us build us a city and a tower, whose top may reach unto heaven; and let us make us a name, lest we be scattered abroad upon the face of the whole earth. **5 And the LORD came down to see the city and the tower, which the children of men builded. 6 And the LORD said, Behold, the people is one and they have all one language; and this they begin to do: and now nothing will be restrained from them, which they have imagined to do. 7 Go to, let us go down and there confound their language, that they may not understand one another's speech.** 8 So the LORD scattered them abroad from thence upon the face of all the earth: and they left off to build the city. **9 Therefore is the name of it called Babel; because the LORD did there confound the language of all the earth:** and from thence did the LORD scatter them abroad upon the face of all the earth.

Exodus 3:

13 And Moses said unto God, Behold, when I come unto the children of Israel and shall say unto them, The God of your fathers hath sent me unto you; and they shall say to me, What is his name? what shall I say unto them? **14 And God said unto Moses, I AM THAT I AM:** and he said, Thus shalt thou say unto the children of Israel, **I AM hath sent me**

unto you. [15]And God said moreover unto Moses, Thus shalt thou say unto the children of Israel, the LORD God of your fathers, the God of Abraham, the God of Isaac and the God of Jacob, hath sent me unto you: **this is my name for ever**, and this is my memorial unto all generations.

Exodus 4:

[11]And the LORD said unto him, Who hath made man's mouth? or who maketh the dumb or deaf or the seeing or the blind? have not I the LORD? **[12]Now therefore go and I will be with thy mouth and teach thee what thou shalt say.** [15]And thou shalt speak unto him and put words in his mouth: and **I will be with thy mouth and with his mouth** and will teach you what ye shall do.

Exodus 20:

[1]And God spake all these words, saying, **[2]I AM the LORD thy God**, which have brought thee out of the land of Egypt, out of the house of bondage. [3]Thou shalt have no other gods before me. **[7]Thou shalt not take the name of the LORD thy God in vain;** for the LORD will not hold him guiltless that taketh his name in vain.

Numbers 22:

[35]And the angel of the LORD said unto Balaam, Go with the men: but **only the word that I shall speak** unto thee, that thou shalt speak. So Balaam went with the princes of Balak.

Deuteronomy 6:

[5]And thou shalt love the LORD thy God with all thine heart and with all thy soul and with all thy might. **[6]And these words, which I command thee this day, shall be in thine heart:**

Deuteronomy 8:

[3]And he humbled thee and suffered thee to hunger and fed thee with manna, which thou knewest not, neither did thy fathers know; that he might make thee know **that man doth not live by bread only, but by every word that proceedeth out of the mouth of the LORD doth man live.**

Deuteronomy 18:

[18]I will raise them up a Prophet from among their brethren, like unto thee and will put my words in his mouth; and he shall speak unto them all that I shall command him. [19]And it shall come to pass, that whosoever will not hearken unto my words which he shall speak in my name, I will require it of him. [20]But the prophet, which shall presume to speak a word in my name, which I have not commanded him to speak or that shall speak in the name of other gods, even that prophet shall die. [21]And if thou say in thine heart, How shall we know the word which the LORD hath not spoken? **[22]When a prophet speaketh in the name of the LORD, if the thing follow not, nor come to pass, that is the thing which the LORD hath not spoken, but the prophet hath spoken it presumptuously: thou shalt not be afraid of him.**

Deuteronomy 30:

[14]But the word is very nigh unto thee, in thy mouth and in thy heart, that thou mayest do it.

Joshua 21:

45 There failed not ought of any good thing which the LORD had spoken unto the house of Israel; all came to pass.

Joshua 24:

15 And if it seem evil unto you to serve the LORD, **choose you this day whom ye will serve;** whether the gods which your fathers served that were on the other side of the flood or the gods of the Amorites, in whose land ye dwell: but as for me and my house, we will serve the LORD.

2 Samuel 23:

2 The Spirit of the LORD spake by me and his word was in my tongue.

Job22:

28 Thou shalt also decree a thing and it shall be established unto thee: and the light shall shine upon thy ways.

Job 27:

3 All the while my breath is in me
and **the spirit of God is in my nos-
trils;** 4 My lips shall not speak
wickedness, nor my tongue utter
deceit.

Psalms 17:

1 Hear the right, O LORD, attend
unto my cry, give ear unto my
prayer, that goeth not out of feigned
lips. **2 Let my sentence come forth
from thy presence;** let thine eyes
behold the things that are equal.
3 Thou hast proved mine heart; thou
hast visited me in the night; thou
hast tried me and shalt find nothing;
I am purposed that my mouth shall
not transgress. 4 Concerning the
works of men, **by the word of thy
lips I have kept me from the paths
of the destroyer.**

Psalms 23:

1 The LORD is my shepherd; I shall not want.

Psalms 33:

4 For the word of the LORD is right;
and all his works are done in truth.
5 He loveth righteousness and judgment: the earth is full of the good-
ness of the LORD. **6 By the word of
the LORD were the heavens made;
and all the host of them by the
breath of his mouth.**

9 For he spake and it was done; he commanded and it stood fast.

Psalms 34:

1 I will bless the LORD at all times: his praise shall continually be in my mouth.

13 Keep thy tongue from evil and thy lips from speaking guile.

Psalms 35:

28 And my tongue shall speak of thy righteousness and of thy praise all the day long.

Psalms 37:

30 The mouth of the righteous speaketh wisdom and his tongue talketh of judgment.

Psalms 39:

1 I said, I will take heed to my ways, that I sin not with my tongue: I will keep my mouth with a bridle, while the wicked is before me.

Psalms 40:

**3 And he hath put a new song in
my mouth,** even praise unto our
God: many shall see it and fear and
shall trust in the LORD. 8 I delight to
do thy will, O my God: yea, thy law
is within my heart. 9 I have preached
righteousness in the great congrega-

tion: lo, I have not refrained my lips, O LORD, thou knowest. 10I have not hid thy righteousness within my heart; I have declared thy faithfulness and thy salvation: I have not concealed thy loving kindness and thy truth from the great congregation.

Psalms 46:

10Be still and know that I AM God:

Psalms 59:

12For the sin of their mouth and the words of their lips let them even be taken in their pride: and for cursing and lying which they speak.

Psalms 119:

2Blessed are they that keep his testimonies and that seek him with the whole heart. 11Thy word have I hid in mine heart, that I might not sin against thee. 3With my lips have I declared all the judgments of thy mouth. 6I will delight myself in thy statutes: I will not forget thy word. **72The law of thy mouth is better unto me than thousands of gold and silver.**

74They that fear thee will be glad when they see me; because I have hoped in thy word. 103How sweet are thy words unto my taste! yea, sweeter than honey to my mouth! 105Thy word is a lamp unto my feet and a light unto my path. 108Accept, I beseech thee, the freewill offerings of my mouth, O LORD and teach me thy judgments. 114Thou art my hiding place and my shield: I hope in thy word. 116Uphold me according unto thy word, that I may live: and let me not be ashamed of my hope.

130The entrance of thy words giveth light; it giveth understanding unto the simple. 140Thy word is very pure: therefore thy servant loveth it. 160Thy word is true from the beginning: and every one of thy righteous judgments endureth for ever. 161Princes have persecuted me without a cause: but **my heart standeth in awe of thy word.** 162I rejoice at thy word, as one that findeth great spoil. 171My lips shall utter praise, when thou hast taught me thy statutes. 172My tongue shall speak of thy word: for all thy commandments are righteousness.

Psalms 139:

4For there is not a word in my tongue, but, lo, O LORD, thou knowest it altogether.

Psalms 141:

3Set a watch, O LORD, before my mouth; keep the door of my lips.

Psalms 145:

21My mouth shall speak the praise of the LORD: and let all flesh bless his holy name for ever and ever.

Proverbs 1:

23Turn you at my reproof: behold, I will pour out my spirit unto you, I will make known my words unto you.

Proverbs 2:

1My son, if thou wilt receive my words and hide my commandments with thee; 2So that thou incline thine ear unto wisdom and apply thine heart to understanding; 3Yea, if thou criest after knowledge and liftest up thy voice for understanding; 4If thou seekest her as silver and searchest for her as for hid treasures; 5Then shalt thou understand the fear of the LORD and find the knowledge of God. 6For the LORD giveth wisdom: out of his mouth cometh knowledge and understanding.

Proverbs 4:

[20]My son, attend to my words; incline thine ear unto my sayings.

[21]Let them not depart from thine eyes; keep them in the midst of thine heart. [22]For they are life unto those that find them and health to all their flesh. **[23]Keep thy heart with all diligence; for out of it are the issues of life**. [24]Put away from thee a forward mouth and perverse lips put far from thee.

Proverbs 5:

[1]My son, attend unto my wisdom and bow thine ear to my understanding: [2]That thou mayest regard discretion and that thy lips may keep knowledge. [7]Hear me now therefore, O ye children and depart not from the words of my mouth.

Proverbs 6:

[2]Thou art snared with the words of thy mouth, thou art taken with the words of thy mouth. [17]A proud look, a lying tongue and hands that shed innocent blood, [18]An heart that deviseth wicked imaginations, feet that be swift in running to mischief, [19]A false witness that speaketh lies and he that soweth discord among brethren.

Proverbs 7:

[1]My son, keep my words and lay up my commandments with thee.

Proverbs 8:

[6]Hear; for I will speak of excellent things; and the opening of my lips shall be right things. [7]For my mouth shall speak truth; and wickedness is an abomination to my lips. [8]All the words of my mouth are in righteousness; there is nothing forward or perverse in them. [9]They are all plain to him that understandeth and right to them that find knowledge. [14]Counsel is mine and sound wisdom: I am understanding; I have strength.

Proverbs 10:

[11]The mouth of a righteous man is a well of life: but violence covereth the mouth of the wicked. [13]In the lips of him that hath understanding wisdom is found: but a rod is for the back of him that is void of understanding. [18]He that hideth hatred with lying lips and he that uttereth a slander, is a fool. [19]In the multitude of words there wanteth not sin: but he that refraineth his lips is wise. **[20]The tongue of the just is as choice silver:** the heart of the wicked is little worth. **[21]The lips of the righteous feed many:** but fools die for want of wisdom. **[31]The mouth of the just bringeth forth wisdom:** but the forward tongue shall be cut out. **[32]The lips of the righteous know what is acceptable:** but the mouth of the wicked speaketh perverseness

Proverbs 11:

[9]An hypocrite with his mouth destroyeth his neighbor: but through knowledge shall the just be delivered. [11]By the blessing of the upright the city is exalted: but it is overthrown by the mouth of the wicked.

Proverbs 12:

[13]The wicked is snared by the transgression of his lips: but the just shall come out of trouble. **[14]A man shall be satisfied with good by the fruit of his mouth:** and the recompense of a man's hands shall be rendered unto him. [17]He that speaketh truth sheweth forth righteousness: but a false witness deceit. [18]There is that speaketh like the piercings of a

sword: but **the tongue of the wise is health.** **19The lip of truth shall be established for ever:** but a lying tongue is but for a moment. 20Deceit is in the heart of them that imagine evil: but to the counselors of peace is joy. 22Lying lips are abomination to the LORD: but they that deal truly are his delight. **25Heaviness in the heart of man maketh it stoop: but a good word maketh it glad.**

Proverbs 13:

2A man shall eat good by the fruit of his mouth: but the soul of the transgressors shall eat violence. **3He that keepeth his mouth keepeth his life:** but he that openeth wide his lips shall have destruction. 5A righteous man hateth lying: but a wicked man is loathsome and cometh to shame. 13Whoso despiseth the word shall be destroyed: but he that feareth the commandment shall be rewarded.

Proverbs 14:

3In the mouth of the foolish is a rod of pride: but **the lips of the wise shall preserve them.** 23In all labor there is profit: but the talk of the lips tendeth only to penury. 25A true witness delivereth souls: but a deceitful witness speaketh lies. 29He that is slow to wrath is of great understanding: but he that is hasty of spirit exalteth folly. **30A sound heart is the life of the flesh: but envy the rottenness of the bones.**

Proverbs 15:

4A wholesome tongue is a tree of life: but perverseness therein is a breach in the spirit. 7The lips of the wise disperse knowledge: but the heart of the foolish doeth not so. 8The sacrifice of the wicked is an abomination to the LORD: but the prayer of the upright is his delight. **13A merry heart maketh a cheerful countenance:** but by sorrow of the heart the spirit is broken. 14The heart of him that hath understanding seeketh knowledge: but the mouth of fools feedeth on foolishness. **23A man hath joy by the answer of his mouth: and a word spoken in due season, how good is it!** 26The thoughts of the wicked are an abomination to the LORD: **but the words of the pure are pleasant words.** **30The light of the eyes rejoiceth the heart: and a good report maketh the bones fat.**

Proverbs 16:

1The preparations of the heart in man and the answer of the tongue, is from the LORD. 3Commit thy works unto the LORD and thy thoughts shall be established. 10A divine sentence is in the lips of the king: his mouth transgresseth not in judgment. **13Righteous lips are the delight of kings; and they love him that speaketh right.** **23The heart of the wise teacheth his mouth and addeth learning to his lips.** **24Pleasant words are as an honeycomb, sweet to the soul and health to the bones.** 26He that laboureth, laboureth for himself; for his mouth craveth it of him. 27An ungodly man diggeth up evil: and in his lips there is as a burning fire. 28A forward man soweth strife: and a whisperer separateth chief friends. 30He shutteth his eyes to devise forward things: moving his lips he bringeth evil to pass. 32He that is slow to anger is better than the mighty; and he that ruleth his spirit than he that taketh a city.

Proverbs 17:

[4]A wicked doer giveth heed to false lips; and a liar giveth ear to a naughty tongue.

[7]Excellent speech becometh not a fool: much less do lying lips a prince.

[20]He that hath a forward heart findeth no good: and he that hath a perverse tongue falleth into mischief.

[27]He that hath knowledge spareth his words: and a man of understanding is of an excellent spirit. [28]Even a fool, when he holdeth his peace, is counted wise: and he that shutteth his lips is esteemed a man of understanding.

Proverbs 18:

[4]The words of a man's mouth are as deep waters and the wellspring of wisdom as a flowing brook. [6]A fool's lips enter into contention and his mouth calleth for strokes. [7]A fool's mouth is his destruction and his lips are the snare of his soul. [8]The words of a talebearer are as wounds and they go down into the innermost parts of the belly. [13]He that answereth a matter before he heareth it, it is folly and shame unto him. **[15]The heart of the prudent getteth knowledge; and the ear of the wise seeketh knowledge. [20]A man's belly shall be satisfied with the fruit of his mouth; and with the increase of his lips shall he be filled. [21]Death and life are in the power of the tongue: and they that love it shall eat the fruit thereof.**

Proverbs 19:

[1]Better is the poor that walketh in his integrity, than he that is perverse in his lips and is a fool. [5]A false witness shall not be unpunished and he that speaketh lies shall not escape. [7]All the brethren of the poor do hate him: how much more do his friends go far from him? he pursueth them with words, yet they are wanting to him. [9]A false witness shall not be unpunished and he that speaketh lies shall perish. [27]Cease, my son, to hear the instruction that causeth to err from the words of knowledge. [28]An ungodly witness scorneth judgment: and the mouth of the wicked devoureth iniquity.

Proverbs 20:

[15]There is gold and a multitude of rubies: but the lips of knowledge are a precious jewel. [17]Bread of deceit is sweet to a man; but afterwards his mouth shall be filled with gravel. [19]He that goeth about as a talebearer revealeth secrets: therefore meddle not with him that flattereth with his lips. [20]Whoso curseth his father or his mother, his lamp shall be put out in obscure darkness. [22]Say not thou, I will recompense evil; but wait on the LORD and he shall save thee. [27]The spirit of man is the candle of the LORD, searching all the inward parts of the belly.

Proverbs 21:

[6]The getting of treasures by a lying tongue is a vanity tossed to and fro of them that seek death. **[23]Whoso keepeth his mouth and his tongue keepeth his soul from troubles.**

Proverbs 22:

[11]He that loveth pureness of heart, for the grace of his lips the king shall be his friend. [12]The eyes of the LORD preserve knowledge and he overthroweth the words of the transgressor.

[17]Bow down thine ear and hear the
words of the wise and apply thine
heart unto my knowledge. [18]For it is
a pleasant thing if thou keep them
within thee; they shall withal be fit-
ted in thy lips. [20]Have not I written to
thee excellent things in counsels and
knowledge, [21]That I might make thee
know the certainty of the words of
truth; that thou mightiest answer the
words of truth to them that send
unto thee?

Proverbs 23:

[7]For as he thinketh in his heart, so is
he: [8]The morsel which thou hast
eaten shalt thou vomit up and lose
thy sweet words. [9]Speak not in the
ears of a fool: for he will despise the
wisdom of thy words. **[12]Apply thine**
heart unto instruction and thine
ears to the words of knowledge.
[16]Yea, my heart shall rejoice, when
thy lips speak right things. [23]Buy the
truth and sell it not; also wisdom
and instruction and understanding.

Proverbs 24:

[26]Every man shall kiss his lips that
giveth a right answer. [28]Be not a witness against thy neighbor without
cause; and deceive not with thy lips.

Proverbs 25:

[2]It is the glory of God to conceal a
thing: but the honor of kings is to
search out a matter. **[11]A word fitly**
spoken is like apples of gold in pic-
tures of silver. [12]As an earring of
gold and an ornament of fine gold,
so is a wise reprover upon an obedient ear.

Proverbs 26:

[22]The words of a talebearer are as
wounds and they go down into the
innermost parts of the belly.
[23]Burning lips and a wicked heart are
like a potsherd covered with silver
dross. [24]He that hateth dissembleth
with his lips and layeth up deceit
within him; [25]When he speaketh fair,
believe him not: for there are seven
abominations in his heart. [26]Whose
hatred is covered by deceit, his
wickedness shall be shewed before
the whole congregation. [28]A lying
tongue hateth those that are afflicted
by it; and a flattering mouth worketh
ruin.

Proverbs 27:

[2]Let another man praise thee and
not thine own mouth; a stranger and
not thine own lips.

Proverbs 29:

[18]Where there is no vision, the people perish: but he that keepeth the
law, happy is he. [19]A servant will not
be corrected by words: for though he
understand he will not answer.
[20]Seest thou a man that is hasty in his
words? there is more hope of a fool
than of him.

Proverbs 30:

[5]Every word of God is pure: he is a
shield unto them that put their trust
in him. [6]Add thou not unto his
words, lest he reprove thee and thou
be found a liar.

Ecclesiastes 5:

[2]Be not rash with thy mouth and let
not thine heart be hasty to utter any
thing before God: for God is in heav-
en and thou upon earth: therefore **let**
thy words be few.

Ecclesiastes 8:

[4]Where the word of a king is, there
is power: and who may say unto
him, What doest thou?

Ecclesiastes 10:

[12]**The words of a wise man's mouth are gracious;** but the lips of a fool will swallow up himself.

Ecclesiastes 12:

[11]The words of the wise are as goads and as nails fastened by the masters of assemblies, which are given from one shepherd.

Isaiah 6:

[5]Then said I, Woe is me! for I am undone; because I am a man of unclean lips and I dwell in the midst of a people of unclean lips: for mine eyes have seen the King, the LORD of hosts. [6]**Then flew one of the seraphims unto me, having a live coal in his hand, which he had taken with the tongs from off the altar: [7]And he laid it upon my mouth and said, Lo, this hath touched thy lips; and thine iniquity is taken away and thy sin purged.**

Isaiah 8:

[10]Take counsel together and it shall come to naught; speak the word and it shall not stand: for God is with us. [20]To the law and to the testimony: if they speak not according to this word, it is because there is no light in them.

Isaiah 10:

[1]Woe unto them that decree unrighteous decrees and that write grievousness which they have prescribed;

Isaiah 14:

[12]How art thou fallen from heaven, O Lucifer, son of the morning! how art thou cut down to the ground, which didst weaken the nations! [13]For thou hast said in thine heart, I will ascend into heaven, I will exalt my throne above the stars of God: I will sit also upon the mount of the congregation, in the sides of the north: [14]**I will ascend above the heights of the clouds; I will be like the most High. [15]Yet thou shalt be brought down to hell, to the sides of the pit.**

Isaiah 43:

[10]Ye are my witnesses, saith the LORD and my servant whom I have chosen: that ye may know and believe me and understand that I AM he: before me there was no God formed, neither shall there be after me. [11]I, even I, AM the LORD; and beside me there is no savior. [12]I have declared and have saved and I have shewed, when there was no strange god among you: therefore ye are my witnesses, saith the LORD, that I AM God. [13]Yea, before the day was I AM he; and there is none that can deliver out of my hand: I will work and who shall let it? [18]Remember ye not the former things, neither consider the things of old. [19]Behold, I will do a new thing; now it shall spring forth; shall ye not know it? I will even make a way in the wilderness and rivers in the desert. [25]I, even I, AM he that blotteth out thy transgressions for mine own sake and will not remember thy sins.

Isaiah 44:

[6]Thus saith the LORD the King of Israel and his redeemer the LORD of hosts; **I AM the first and I AM the last; and beside me there is no God.** [7]And who, as I, shall call and shall declare it and set it in order for me, since I appointed the ancient people? and the things that are coming and

shall come, let them shew unto them. 8Fear ye not, neither be afraid: have not I told thee from that time and have declared it? ye are even my witnesses. Is there a God beside me? yea, there is no God; I know not any.

Isaiah 45:

5I AM the LORD and there is none else, there is no God beside me: I girded thee, though thou hast not known me: 6That they may know from the rising of the sun and from the west, that there is none beside me. I AM the LORD and there is none else.

7I form the light and create darkness: I make peace and create evil: I the LORD do all these things. 8Drop down, ye heavens, from above and let the skies pour down righteousness: let the earth open and let them bring forth salvation and let righteousness spring up together; I the LORD have created it.

18For thus saith the LORD that created the heavens; God himself that formed the earth and made it; he hath established it, he created it not in vain, he formed it to be inhabited: I AM the LORD; and there is none else. 19I have not spoken in secret, in a dark place of the earth: I said not unto the seed of Jacob, Seek ye me in vain: I the LORD speak righteousness, **I declare things that are right.** 22Look unto me and be ye saved, all the ends of the earth: for I AM God and there is none else. 23I have sworn by myself, **the word is gone out of my mouth in righteousness and shall not return, That unto me every knee shall bow, every tongue shall swear.**

Isaiah 46:

9Remember the former things of old: for I AM God and there is none else; I AM God and there is none like me, 10Declaring the end from the beginning and from ancient times the things that are not yet done, saying, My counsel shall stand and I will do all my pleasure: 11Calling a ravenous bird from the east, the man that executeth my counsel from a far country: yea, I have spoken it, I will also bring it to pass; I have purposed it, I will also do it.

Isaiah 48:

3I have declared the former things from the beginning; and they went forth out of my mouth and I shewed them; I did them suddenly and they came to pass. 12Hearken unto me, O Jacob and Israel, my called; I AM he; I AM the first, I also AM the last. 17Thus saith the LORD, thy Redeemer, the Holy One of Israel; I AM the LORD thy God which teacheth thee to profit, which leadeth thee by the way that thou shouldest go.

Isaiah 50:

4The Lord GOD hath given me the tongue of the learned, that I should know how to speak a word in season to him that is weary: he wakeneth morning by morning, he wakeneth mine ear to hear as the learned. 5The Lord GOD hath opened mine ear and I was not rebellious, neither turned away back.

Isaiah 51:

12I, even I, AM he that comforteth you: who art thou, that thou shouldest be afraid of a man that shall die and of the son of man which shall be made as grass; 16 And

I have put my words in thy mouth and I have covered thee in the shadow of mine hand, that I may plant the heavens and lay the foundations of the earth and say unto Zion, Thou art my people.

Isaiah 52:

[6]Therefore my people shall know my name: therefore they shall know in that day that I AM he that doth speak: behold, it is I.

Isaiah 55:

[3]Incline your ear and come unto me: hear and your soul shall live; and I will make an everlasting covenant with you, even the sure mercies of David. [11]**So shall my word be that goeth forth out of my mouth: it shall not return unto me void, but it shall accomplish that which I please and it shall prosper in the thing whereto I sent it.**

Isaiah 58:

[9]Then shalt thou call and the LORD shall answer; thou shalt cry and he shall say, Here I AM. If thou take away from the midst of thee the yoke, the putting forth of the finger and speaking vanity;

Isaiah 61:

[1]The Spirit of the Lord GOD is upon me; because the LORD hath anointed me to preach good tidings unto the meek; he hath sent me to bind up the brokenhearted, to proclaim liberty to the captives and the opening of the prison to them that are bound;

Isaiah 65:

[24]And it shall come to pass, that before they call, I will answer; and while they are yet speaking, I will hear.

Jeremiah 1:

[6]Then said I, Ah, Lord GOD! behold, I cannot speak: for I am a child. [7]But the LORD said unto me, Say not, I am a child: for thou shalt go to all that I shall send thee and whatsoever I command thee thou shalt speak. [8]Be not afraid of their faces: for I AM with thee to deliver thee, saith the LORD. [9]Then the LORD put forth his hand and touched my mouth. And the LORD said unto me, Behold, I have put my words in thy mouth. [10]See, I have this day set thee over the nations and over the kingdoms, to root out and to pull down and to destroy and to throw down, to build and to plant.

Jeremiah 7:

[8]Behold, ye trust in lying words, that cannot profit.

Jeremiah 15:

[16]Thy words were found and I did eat them; and thy word was unto me the joy and rejoicing of mine heart: for I AM called by thy name, O LORD God of hosts.

Ezekiel 28:

[1]The word of the LORD came again unto me, saying,

[2]Son of man, say unto the prince of Tyrus, Thus saith the Lord GOD; Because thine heart is lifted up and thou hast said, I am a God, I sit in the seat of God, in the midst of the seas; yet thou art a man and not God, though thou set thine heart as the heart of God:

Ezekiel 37:

[3]And he said unto me, Son of man, can these bones live? And I answered, O Lord GOD, thou knowest. [4]Again he said unto me,

Prophesy upon these bones and say
unto them, O ye dry bones, hear the
word of the LORD. [5]Thus saith the
Lord GOD unto these bones; Behold,
I will cause breath to enter into you
and ye shall live: [6]And I will lay
sinews upon you and will bring up
flesh upon you and cover you with
skin and put breath in you and ye
shall live; and ye shall know that I
AM the LORD. [7]So I prophesied as I
was commanded: and as I prophesied, there was a noise and behold a
shaking and the bones came together, bone to his bone. [8]And when I
beheld, lo, the sinews and the flesh
came up upon them and the skin
covered them above: but there was
no breath in them. [9]Then said he
unto me, Prophesy unto the wind,
prophesy, son of man and say to the
wind, Thus saith the Lord GOD;
Come from the four winds, O breath
and breathe upon these slain, that
they may live. [10]So I prophesied as he
commanded me and the breath
came into them and they lived and
stood up upon their feet, an exceed-
ing great army. [11]Then he said unto
me, Son of man, these bones are the
whole house of Israel: behold, they
say, Our bones are dried and our
hope is lost: we are cut off for our
parts. [12]Therefore prophesy and say
unto them, Thus saith the Lord
GOD; Behold, O my people, I will
open your graves and cause you to
come up out of your graves and
bring you into the land of Israel.
[13]And ye shall know that I AM the
LORD, when I have opened your
graves, O my people and brought
you up out of your graves, [14]And
shall put my spirit in you and ye
shall live and I shall place you in
your own land: then shall ye know
that I the LORD have spoken it and
performed it, saith the LORD.

Joel 2:

[27]And ye shall know that I AM in
the midst of Israel and that I AM the
LORD your God and none else: and
my people shall never be ashamed.
[28]And it shall come to pass afterward, that **I will pour out my spirit
upon all flesh; and your sons and
your daughters shall prophesy,
your old men shall dream dreams,
your young men shall see visions:**
[29]And also upon the servants and
upon the handmaids in those days
will I pour out my spirit. **[32]And it
shall come to pass, that whosoever
shall call on the name of the LORD
shall be delivered:** for in mount
Zion and in Jerusalem shall be deliv-
erance, as the LORD hath said and in
the remnant whom the LORD shall
call.

Joel 3:

[10]Beat your plowshares into swords
and your pruning hooks into spears:
let the weak say, I AM strong.

Habakkuk 2:

[3]For the vision is yet for an appointed time, but at the end it shall speak
and not lie: though it tarry, wait for
it; because it will surely come, it will
not tarry. [4]Behold, his soul which is
lifted up is not upright in him: but
the just shall live by his faith.

Zephaniah 3:

[9]For then will I turn to the people a
pure language, that they may all call
upon the name of the LORD, to
serve him with one consent. [10]From
beyond the rivers of Ethiopia my
suppliants, even the daughter of my
dispersed, shall bring mine offering.

[11]In that day shalt thou not be ashamed for all thy doings, wherein thou hast transgressed against me: for then I will take away out of the midst of thee them that rejoice in thy pride and thou shalt no more be haughty because of my holy mountain. [12]I will also leave in the midst of thee an afflicted and poor people and they shall trust in the name of the LORD. [13]The remnant of Israel shall not do iniquity, nor speak lies; neither shall a deceitful tongue be found in their mouth: for they shall feed and lie down and none shall make them afraid. [14]Sing, O daughter of Zion; shout, O Israel; be glad and rejoice with all the heart, O daughter of Jerusalem. [15]The LORD hath taken away thy judgments, he hath cast out thine enemy: the king of Israel, even the LORD, is in the midst of thee: thou shalt not see evil any more. [16]In that day it shall be said to Jerusalem, Fear thou not: and to Zion, Let not thine hands be slack. [17]The LORD thy God in the midst of thee is mighty; he will save, he will rejoice over thee with joy; he will rest in his love, he will joy over thee with singing. [18]I will gather them that are sorrowful for the solemn assembly, who are of thee, to whom the reproach of it was a burden. [19]Behold, at that time I will undo all that afflict thee: and I will save her that halteth and gather her that was driven out; and I will get them praise and fame in every land where they have been put to shame. [20]At that time will I bring you again, even in the time that I gather you: for I will make you a name and a praise among all people of the earth, when I turn back your captivity before your eyes, saith the LORD.

Zechariah 8:

[16]These are the things that ye shall do; Speak ye every man the truth to his neighbor; execute the judgment of truth and peace in your gates: [17]And let none of you imagine evil in your hearts against his neighbor; and love no false oath: for all these are things that I hate, saith the LORD.

Matthew 3:

[17]And lo a voice from heaven, saying, This is my beloved Son, in whom I AM well pleased.

Matthew 4:

[4]But he answered and said, It is written, Man shall not live by bread alone, but by every word that proceedeth out of the mouth of God.

Matthew 5:

[14]Ye are the light of the world. A city that is set on an hill cannot be hid. [15]Neither do men light a candle and put it under a bushel, but on a candlestick; and it giveth light unto all that are in the house. **[16]Let your light so shine before men, that they may see your good works and glorify your Father which is in heaven.** [17]Think not that I AM come to destroy the law or the prophets: I AM not come to destroy, but to fulfill. [18]For verily I say unto you, Till heaven and earth pass, one jot or one title shall in no wise pass from the law, till all be fulfilled. [44]But I say unto you, **Love your enemies, bless them that curse you, do good to them that hate you and pray for them which despitefully use you and persecute you; [48]Be ye therefore perfect, even as your Father which is in heaven is perfect.**

Matthew 6:

[1]Take heed that ye do not your alms before men, to be seen of them: otherwise ye have no reward of your Father which is in heaven. [2]Therefore when thou doest thine alms, do not sound a trumpet before thee, as the hypocrites do in the synagogues and in the streets, that they may have glory of men. Verily I say unto you, They have their reward. [3]But when thou doest alms, let not thy left hand know what thy right hand doeth: **[4]That thine alms may be in secret: and thy Father which seeth in secret himself shall reward thee openly.** [5]And when thou prayest, thou shalt not be as the hypocrites are: for they love to pray standing in the synagogues and in the corners of the streets, that they may be seen of men. Verily I say unto you, They have their reward. [6]But thou, when thou prayest, enter into thy closet and when thou hast shut thy door, pray to thy Father which is in secret; and thy Father which seeth in secret shall reward thee openly. [7]But when ye pray, use not vain repetitions, as the heathen do: for they think that they shall be heard for their much speaking. [8]Be not ye therefore like unto them: for your Father knoweth what things ye have need of, before ye ask him. **[9]After this manner therefore pray ye: Our Father which art in heaven, Hallowed be thy name. [10]Thy kingdom come, Thy will be done in earth, as it is in heaven. [11]Give us this day our daily bread. [12]And forgive us our debts, as we forgive our debtors. [13]And lead us not into temptation, but deliver us from evil: For thine is the kingdom and the power and the glory, for ever. Amen.**

[14]For if ye forgive men their trespasses, your heavenly Father will also forgive you: [15]But if ye forgive not men their trespasses, neither will your Father forgive your trespasses.

[21]For where your treasure is, there will your heart be also. [22]The light of the body is the eye: if therefore thine eye be single, thy whole body shall be full of light. [33]But seek ye first the kingdom of God and his righteousness; and all these things shall be added unto you.

Matthew 7:

[7]Ask and it shall be given you; seek and ye shall find; knock and it shall be opened unto you: [8]For every one that asketh receiveth; and he that seeketh findeth; and to him that knocketh it shall be opened. [9]Or what man is there of you, whom if his son ask bread, will he give him a stone? [10]Or if he ask a fish, will he give him a serpent? [11]If ye then, being evil, know how to give good gifts unto your children, how much more shall your Father which is in heaven give good things to them that ask him? [12]Therefore all things whatsoever ye would that men should do to you, do ye even so to them: for this is the law and the prophets. [20]Wherefore by their fruits ye shall know them. [24]Therefore whosoever heareth these sayings of mine and doeth them, I will liken him unto a wise man, which built his house upon a rock:

Matthew 8:

[8]The centurion answered and said, Lord, I am not worthy that thou shouldest come under my roof: **but speak the word only and my ser-**

vant shall be healed. [9]For I AM a man under authority, having soldiers under me: and I say to this man, Go and he goeth; and to another, Come and he cometh; and to my servant, Do this and he doeth it. [10]When Jesus heard it, he marveled and said to them that followed, Verily I say unto you, I have not found so great faith, no, not in Israel. [13]And Jesus said unto the centurion, Go thy way; and **as thou hast believed, so be it done unto thee.** And his servant was healed in the selfsame hour.

Matthew 10:

[16]Behold, I send you forth as sheep in the midst of wolves: be ye therefore wise as serpents and harmless as doves. [19]But when they deliver you up, take no thought how or what ye shall speak: for it shall be given you in that same hour what ye shall speak. [20]For it is not ye that speak, but the Spirit of your Father which speaketh in you. [32]Whosoever therefore shall confess me before men, him will I confess also before my Father which is in heaven. [33]But whosoever shall deny me before men, him will I also deny before my Father which is in heaven. [34]Think not that I AM come to send peace on earth: I came not to send peace, but a sword.

Matthew 12:

[31]Wherefore I say unto you, All manner of sin and blasphemy shall be forgiven unto men: but the blasphemy against the Holy Ghost shall not be forgiven unto men. [32]And whosoever speaketh a word against the Son of man, it shall be forgiven him: but whosoever speaketh against the Holy Ghost, it shall not be forgiven him, neither in this world, neither in the world to come. [33]Either make the tree good and his fruit good; or else make the tree corrupt and his fruit corrupt: for the tree is known by his fruit. [34]O generation of vipers, how can ye, being evil, speak good things? **for out of the abundance of the heart the mouth speaketh. [35]A good man out of the good treasure of the heart bringeth forth good things:** and an evil man out of the evil treasure bringeth forth evil things. **[36]But I say unto you, That every idle word that men shall speak, they shall give account thereof in the day of judgment. [37]For by thy words thou shalt be justified and by thy words thou shalt be condemned.**

Matthew 13:

[18]Hear ye therefore the parable of the sower. [19]When any one heareth the word of the kingdom and understandeth it not, then cometh the wicked one and catcheth away that which was sown in his heart. This is he which received seed by the way side. [20]But he that received the seed into stony places, the same is he that heareth the word and immediately with joy receiveth it;

[21]Yet hath he not root in himself, but dureth for a while: for when tribulation or persecution ariseth because of the word, by and by he is offended. [22]He also that received seed among the thorns is he that heareth the word; and the care of this world and the deceitfulness of riches, choke the word and he becometh unfruitful. **[23]But he that received seed into the good ground is he that heareth the word and understandeth it; which also beareth fruit and**

bringeth forth, some an hundred-
fold, some sixty, some thirty. 34All
these things spake Jesus unto the
multitude in parables; and without a
parable spake he not unto them:
35That it might be fulfilled which was
spoken by the prophet, saying, I will
open my mouth in parables; I will
utter things which have been kept
secret from the foundation of the
world.

Matthew 16:

19And I will give unto thee the keys
of the kingdom of heaven: and whatsoever thou shalt bind on earth shall
be bound in heaven: and whatsoever thou shalt loose on earth shall be
loosed in heaven.

Matthew 17:

20And Jesus said unto them,
Because of your unbelief: for verily I
say unto you, If ye have faith as a
grain of mustard seed, ye shall say
unto this mountain, Remove hence
to yonder place; and it shall remove;
and nothing shall be impossible unto
you.

21Howbeit this kind goeth not out
but by prayer and fasting.

Matthew 21:

21Jesus answered and said unto
them, Verily I say unto you, If ye
have faith and doubt not, ye shall
not only do this which is done to the
fig tree, but also **if ye shall say unto**
this mountain, Be thou removed
and be thou cast into the sea; it shall
be done. 22And all things, whatsoev-
er ye shall ask in prayer, believing,
ye shall receive.

Matthew 22:

36Master, which is the great commandment in the law? 37Jesus said
unto him, Thou shalt love the Lord
thy God with all thy heart and with
all thy soul and with all thy mind.
38This is the first and great commandment. 39And the second is like
unto it, Thou shalt love thy neighbor
as thyself. 40On these two commandments hang all the law and the
prophets.

Matthew 25:

23His lord said unto him, Well done,
good and faithful servant; **thou hast**
been faithful over a few things, I
will make thee ruler over many
things: enter thou into the joy of thy
lord.

Matthew 28:

20Teaching them to observe all
things whatsoever I have commanded you: and, lo, **I AM with you**
always, even unto the end of the
world. Amen.

Mark 4:

14The sower soweth the word.
15And these are they by the way side,
where the word is sown; but when
they have heard, Satan cometh
immediately and taketh away the
word that was sown in their hearts.
16And these are they likewise which
are sown on stony ground; who,
when they have heard the word,
immediately receive it with glad-
ness; 17And have no root in themselves and so endure but for a time:
afterward, when affliction or persecution ariseth for the word's sake,
immediately they are offended.
18And these are they which are sown
among thorns; such as hear the
word, 19And the cares of this world
and the deceitfulness of riches and
the lusts of other things entering in,
choke the word and it becometh

unfruitful. [20]And these are they which are sown on good ground; such as hear the word and receive it and bring forth fruit, some thirty fold, some sixty and some an hundred. [21]And he said unto them, Is a candle brought to be put under a bushel or under a bed? and not to be set on a candlestick? [22]For there is nothing hid, which shall not be manifested; neither was any thing kept secret, but that it should come abroad. **[23]If any man have ears to hear, let him hear.**

[24]And he said unto them, Take heed what ye hear: with what measure ye mete, it shall be measured to you: and unto you that hear shall more be given. [25]For he that hath, to him shall be given: and he that hath not, from him shall be taken even that which he hath.

[39]And he arose and rebuked the wind and said unto the sea, Peace, be still. And the wind ceased and there was a great calm.

[40]And he said unto them, Why are ye so fearful? how is it that ye have no faith?

Mark 7:

[14]And when he had called all the people unto him, he said unto them, Hearken unto me every one of you and understand: [15]There is nothing from without a man, that entering into him can defile him: but the things which come out of him, those are they that defile the man. [16]If any man have ears to hear, let him hear.

[17]And when he was entered into the house from the people, his disciples asked him concerning the parable. [18]And he saith unto them, Are ye so without understanding also? **Do ye not perceive, that whatsoever thing from without entereth into the man, it cannot defile him; [19]Because it entereth not into his heart, but into the belly and goeth out into the draught, purging all meats? [20]And he said, That which cometh out of the man, that defileth the man. [21]For from within, out of the heart of men, proceed evil thoughts, adulteries, fornications, murders, [22]Thefts, covetousness, wickedness, deceit, lasciviousness, an evil eye, blasphemy, pride, foolishness: [23]All these evil things come from within and defile the man.**

Mark 9:

[23]Jesus said unto him, If thou canst believe, all things are possible to him that believeth.

Mark 11:

[22]And Jesus answering saith unto them, Have faith in God. [23]For verily I say unto you, That whosoever shall say unto this mountain, Be thou removed and be thou cast into the sea; and shall not doubt in his heart, but shall believe that those things which he saith shall come to pass; he shall have whatsoever he saith. [24]Therefore I say unto you, What things soever ye desire, when ye pray, believe that ye receive them and ye shall have them.

Luke 4:

[4]And Jesus answered him, saying, It is written, That man shall not live by bread alone, but by every word of God.

Luke 8:

[9]And his disciples asked him, saying, What might this parable be? [10]And he said, Unto you it is given to

know the mysteries of the kingdom of God: but to others in parables; that seeing they might not see and hearing they might not understand. 11 Now the parable is this: **The seed is the word of God. 12 Those by the way side are they that hear; then cometh the devil and taketh away the word out of their hearts, lest they should believe and be saved. 13 They on the rock are they, which, when they hear, receive the word with joy; and these have no root, which for a while believe and in time of temptation fall away. 14 And that which fell among thorns are they, which, when they have heard, go forth and are choked with cares and riches and pleasures of this life and bring no fruit to perfection. 15 But that on the good ground are they, which in an honest and good heart, having heard the word, keep it and bring forth fruit with patience. 16 No man, when he hath lighted a candle, covereth it with a vessel or putteth it under a bed; but setteth it on a candlestick, that they which enter in may see the light. 17 For nothing is secret, that shall not be made manifest; neither any thing hid, that shall not be known and come abroad. 18 Take heed therefore how ye hear: for whosoever hath, to him shall be given; and whosoever hath not, from him shall be taken even that which he seemeth to have.**

Luke 11:

1 And it came to pass, that, as he was praying in a certain place, when he ceased, one of his disciples said unto him, Lord, teach us to pray, as John also taught his disciples. 2 And he said unto them, When ye pray, say, Our Father which art in heaven, Hallowed be thy name. Thy kingdom come. Thy will be done, as in heaven, so in earth. 3 Give us day by day our daily bread.

4 And forgive us our sins; for we also forgive every one that is indebted to us. And lead us not into temptation; but deliver us from evil. 5 And he said unto them, Which of you shall have a friend and shall go unto him at midnight and say unto him, Friend, lend me three loaves; 6 For a friend of mine in his journey is come to me and I have nothing to set before him?

7 And he from within shall answer and say, Trouble me not: the door is now shut and my children are with me in bed; I cannot rise and give thee. 8 I say unto you, Though he will not rise and give him, because he is his friend, yet because of his importunity he will rise and give him as many as he needeth. **9 And I say unto you, Ask and it shall be given you; seek and ye shall find; knock and it shall be opened unto you. 10 For every one that asketh receiveth; and he that seeketh findeth; and to him that knocketh it shall be opened.**

28 But he said, Yea rather, blessed are they that hear the word of God and keep it.

Luke 12:

11 And when they bring you unto the synagogues and unto magistrates and powers, take ye no thought how or what thing ye shall answer or what ye shall say: **12 For the Holy Ghost shall teach you in the same hour what ye ought to say. 31 But rather seek ye the kingdom of God; and all these things shall be**

added unto you. [32]Fear not, little flock; for it is your Father's good pleasure to give you the kingdom. [34]For where your treasure is, there will your heart be also.

Luke 17:

[21]Neither shall they say, Lo here! or, lo there! for, **behold, the kingdom of God is within you.**

Luke 18:

[27]And he said, The things which are impossible with men are possible with God.

Luke 21:

[12]But before all these, they shall lay their hands on you and persecute you, delivering you up to the synagogues and into prisons, being brought before kings and rulers for my name's sake. [13]And it shall turn to you for a testimony. **[14]Settle it therefore in your hearts, not to meditate before what ye shall answer: [15]For I will give you a mouth and wisdom, which all your adversaries shall not be able to gainsay nor resist. [33]Heaven and earth shall pass away: but my words shall not pass away.**

John 1:

[1]In the beginning was the Word and the Word was with God and the Word was God. [2]The same was in the beginning with God. [3]All things were made by him; and without him was not any thing made that was made. [4]In him was life; and the life was the light of men. [5]And the light shineth in darkness; and the darkness comprehended it not. [14]And the Word was made flesh and dwelt among us,-and we beheld his glory, the glory as of the only begotten of the Father,-full of grace and truth.

John 3:

[5]Jesus answered, Verily, verily, I say unto thee, Except a man be born of water and of the Spirit, he cannot enter into the kingdom of God. [6]That which is born of the flesh is flesh; and that which is born of the Spirit is spirit. [34]For he whom God hath sent speaketh the words of God: for God giveth not the Spirit by measure unto him.

John 6:

[35]And Jesus said unto them, I AM the bread of life: he that cometh to me shall never hunger; and he that believeth on me shall never thirst. [43]Jesus therefore answered and said unto them, **Murmur not among yourselves.** [44]No man can come to me, except the Father which hath sent me draw him: and I will raise him up at the last day. [45]It is written in the prophets and they shall be all taught of God. Every man therefore that hath heard and hath learned of the Father, cometh unto me.

[48]I AM that bread of life.

[51]I AM the living bread which came down from heaven: if any man eat of this bread, he shall live for ever: and the bread that I will give is my flesh, which I will give for the life of the world.

[63]It is the spirit that quickeneth; the flesh profiteth nothing: the words that I speak unto you, they are spirit and they are life.

John 7:

[28]Then cried Jesus in the temple as he taught, saying, Ye both know me and ye know whence I AM: and I AM not come of myself, but he that sent me is true, whom ye know not.

29 But I know him: for I AM from him and he hath sent me.

John 8:

12 Then spake Jesus again unto them, saying, I AM the light of the world: he that followeth me shall not walk in darkness, but shall have the light of life.

John 10:

9 I AM the door: by me if any man enter in, he shall be saved and shall go in and out and find pasture. 10 The thief cometh not, but for to steal and to kill and to destroy: I AM come that they might have life and that they might have it more abundantly. 11 I AM the good shepherd: the good shepherd giveth his life for the sheep. 14 I AM the good shepherd and know my sheep and am known of mine. 30 I and my Father are one.

John 14:

1 Let not your heart be troubled: ye believe in God, believe also in me. 2 In my Father's house are many mansions: if it were not so, I would have told you. I go to prepare a place for you. 3 And if I go and prepare a place for you, I will come again and receive you unto myself; **that where I AM, there ye may be also.** 6 Jesus saith unto him, **I AM the way, the truth and the life: no man cometh unto the Father, but by me.** 10 Believest thou not that I AM in the Father and the Father in me? **the words that I speak unto you I speak not of myself: but the Father that dwelleth in me, he doeth the works. 11 Believe me that I AM in the Father and the Father in me: or else believe me for the very works' sake. 12 Verily, verily, I say unto you, He that believeth on me, the works that I do shall he do also; and greater works than these shall he do; because I go unto my Father. 13 And whatsoever ye shall ask in my name, that will I do, that the Father may be glorified in the Son. 14 If ye shall ask any thing in my name, I will do it. 15 If ye love me, keep my commandments.**

16 And I will pray the Father and he shall give you another Comforter, that he may abide with you for ever; 17 Even the Spirit of truth; whom the world cannot receive, because it seeth him not, neither knoweth him: but ye know him; for he dwelleth with you and shall be in you. 18 I will not leave you comfortless: I will come to you. 19 Yet a little while and the world seeth me no more; but ye see me: because I live, ye shall live also. 20 At that day ye shall know that I AM in my Father and ye in me and I in you. 21 He that hath my commandments and keepeth them, he it is that loveth me: and he that loveth me shall be loved of my Father and I will love him and will manifest myself to him. 23 Jesus answered and said unto him, If a man love me, he will keep my words: and my Father will love him and we will come unto him and make our abode with him. 24 He that loveth me not keepeth not my sayings: and the word which ye hear is not mine, but the Father's which sent me. 25 These things have I spoken unto you, being yet present with you. 26 But the Comforter, which is the Holy Ghost, whom the Father will send in my name, he shall teach you all things and bring all things to your remembrance, whatsoever I have said unto you. 27 Peace I leave with you, my peace I give unto you: not as the world giveth, give I unto

you. Let not your heart be troubled, neither let it be afraid.

John 15:

1I AM the true vine and my Father is the husbandman. 2Every branch in me that beareth not fruit he taketh away: and every branch that beareth fruit, he purgeth it, that it may bring forth more fruit. 3Now ye are clean through the word which I have spoken unto you. 4Abide in me and I in you. As the branch cannot bear fruit of itself, except it abide in the vine; no more can ye, except ye abide in me. 5I AM the vine, ye are the branches: He that abideth in me and I in him, the same bringeth forth much fruit: for without me ye can do nothing.

7If ye abide in me and my words abide in you, ye shall ask what ye will and it shall be done unto you.

16Ye have not chosen me, but I have chosen you and ordained you, that ye should go and bring forth fruit and that your fruit should remain: that whatsoever ye shall ask of the Father in my name, he may give it you. 17These things I command you, that ye love one another.

John 16:

12I have yet many things to say unto you, but ye cannot bear them now. 13Howbeit when he, the Spirit of truth, is come, he will guide you into all truth: for he shall not speak of himself; but whatsoever he shall hear, that shall he speak: and he will shew you things to come. 14He shall glorify me: for he shall receive of mine and shall shew it unto you. 15All things that the Father hath are mine: therefore said I, that he shall take of mine and shall shew it unto you.

John 17:

17Sanctify them through thy truth: thy word is truth.

Acts 4:

29And now, Lord, behold their threatenings: and grant unto thy servants, **that with all boldness they may speak thy word,** 30By stretching forth thine hand to heal; and that signs and wonders may be done by the name of thy holy child Jesus. 31And when they had prayed, the place was shaken where they were assembled together; and they were all filled with the Holy Ghost and they spake the word of God with boldness.

Acts 27:

23For there stood by me this night the angel of God, whose I AM and whom I serve, 24Saying, Fear not, Paul; thou must be brought before Caesar: and, lo, God hath given thee all them that sail with thee.

Romans 8:

31What shall we then say to these things? If God be for us, who can be against us?

Romans 10:

8But what saith it? The word is nigh thee, even in thy mouth and in thy heart: that is, the word of faith, which we preach; 9That if thou shalt confess with thy mouth the Lord Jesus and shalt believe in thine heart that God hath raised him from the dead, thou shalt be saved. 10For with the heart man believeth unto righteousness; and with the mouth confession is made unto salvation. **13For whosoever shall call upon the name of the Lord shall be saved. 17So then faith cometh by hearing and hearing by the word of God.**

Romans 12:

2 And be not conformed to this world: but be ye transformed by the renewing of your mind, that ye may prove what is that good and acceptable and perfect, will of God. 12 Rejoicing in hope; patient in tribulation; continuing diligently in prayer;

Romans 14:

11 For it is written, As I live, saith the Lord, every knee shall bow to me and **every tongue shall confess to God.** 16 Let not then your good be evil spoken of: 17 For the kingdom of God is not meat and drink; but righteousness and peace and joy in the Holy Ghost.

Romans 15:

6 That ye may with one mind and one mouth glorify God, even the Father of our Lord Jesus Christ.

1 Corinthians 4:

20 For the kingdom of God is not in word, but in power.

1 Corinthians 10:

15 I speak as to wise men; judge ye what I say.

1 Corinthians 12:

8 For to one is given by the Spirit the word of wisdom; to another the word of knowledge by the same Spirit; 9 To another faith by the same Spirit; to another the gifts of healing by the same Spirit; 10 To another the working of miracles; to another prophecy; to another discerning of spirits; to another divers kinds of tongues; to another the interpretation of tongues: 11 But all these worketh that one and the selfsame Spirit, dividing to every man severally as he will.

1 Corinthians 13:

10 But when that which is perfect is come, then that which is in part shall be done away. 11 When I was a child, I spake as a child, I understood as a child, I thought as a child: but when I became a man, I put away childish things. 12 For now we see through a glass, darkly; but then face to face: now I know in part; but then shall I know even as also I AM known. 13 And now abideth faith, hope, love, these three; but the greatest of these is love.

Galatians 5:

14 For all the law is fulfilled in one word, even in this; Thou shalt love thy neighbor as thyself.

Ephesians 4:

22 That ye put off concerning the former conversation the old man, which is corrupt according to the deceitful lusts; 23 And be renewed in the spirit of your mind; 24 And that ye put on the new man, which after God is created in righteousness and true holiness. 25 Wherefore putting away lying, speak every man truth with his neighbor: for we are members one of another. 29 Let no corrupt communication proceed out of your mouth, but that which is good to the use of edifying, that it may minister grace unto the hearers. 31 Let all bitterness and wrath and anger and clamor and evil speaking, be put away from you, with all malice: 32 And be ye kind one to another, tenderhearted, forgiving one another, even as God for Christ's sake hath forgiven you.

Ephesians 5:

4 Neither filthiness, nor foolish talking, nor jesting, which are not con-

venient: but rather giving of thanks. [6]Let no man deceive you with vain words: for because of these things cometh the wrath of God upon the children of disobedience. [12]For it is a shame even to speak of those things which are done of them in secret.

[19]Speaking to yourselves in psalms and hymns and spiritual songs, singing and making melody in your heart to the Lord;

Ephesians 6:

[18]Praying always with all prayer and supplication in the Spirit and watching thereunto with all perseverance and supplication for all saints; [19]And for me, that utterance may be given unto me, that I may open my mouth boldly, to make known the mystery of the gospel, [20]For which I AM an ambassador in bonds: that therein I may speak boldly, as I ought to speak.

Philippians 2:

[14]Do all things without murmurings and disputings:

[16]Holding forth the word of life; that I may rejoice in the day of Christ, that I have not run in vain, neither labored in vain.

Philippians 4:

[6]Be anxious for nothing; but in every thing by prayer and supplication with thanksgiving let your requests be made known unto God. **[8]Finally, brethren, whatsoever things are true, whatsoever things are honest, whatsoever things are just, whatsoever things are pure, whatsoever things are lovely, whatsoever things are of good report; if there be any virtue and if there be any praise, think on these things.** [11]Not that I speak in respect of want: for I have learned, in whatsoever state I AM, therewith to be content. [12]I know both how to be abased and I know how to abound: every where and in all things I AM instructed both to be full and to be hungry, both to abound and to suffer need. [13]I can do all things through Christ which strengtheneth me.

Colossians 3:

[8]But now ye also put off all these; anger, wrath, malice, blasphemy, filthy communication out of your mouth. [9]Lie not one to another, seeing that ye have put off the old man with his deeds; [10]And have put on the new man, which is renewed in knowledge after the image of him that created him: [17]And whatsoever ye do in word or deed, do all in the name of the Lord Jesus, giving thanks to God and the Father by him. [23]And whatsoever ye do, do it heartily, as to the Lord and not unto men;

Colossians 4:

[4]That I may make it manifest, as I ought to speak. [5]Walk in wisdom toward them that are without, redeeming the time. [6]Let your speech be always with grace, seasoned with salt, that ye may know how ye ought to answer every man.

1 Thessalonians 2:

[4]But as we were allowed of God to be put in trust with the gospel, even so we speak; not as pleasing men, but God, which trieth our hearts. [5]For neither at any time used we flattering words, as ye know, nor a cloke of covetousness; God is witness:

1 Thessalonians 5:

17**Pray without ceasing.** 18In every thing give thanks: for this is the will of God in Christ Jesus concerning you. 19Quench not the Spirit. 20Despise not prophesying. 21**Prove all things; hold fast that which is good.**

2 Thessalonians 2:

17Comfort your hearts and stablish you in every good word and work.

1 Timothy 4:

4For every creature of God is good and nothing to be refused, if it be received with thanksgiving: 5For it is sanctified by the word of God and prayer. 6If thou put the brethren in remembrance of these things, thou shalt be a good minister of Jesus Christ, nourished up in the words of faith and of good doctrine, whereunto thou hast attained.

2 Timothy 1:

13Hold fast the form of sound words, which thou hast heard of me, in faith and love which is in Christ Jesus. 14That good thing which was committed unto thee keep by the Holy Ghost which dwelleth in us.

1 Timothy 2:

15Study to shew thyself approved unto God, a workman that needeth not to be ashamed, rightly dividing the word of truth.

16But shun profane and vain babblings: for they will increase unto more ungodliness. 17And their word will eat as doth a canker: of whom is Hymenaeus and Philetus; 23But foolish and unlearned questions avoid, knowing that they do gender strifes.

Titus 1:

15Unto the pure all things are pure: but unto them that are defiled and unbelieving is nothing pure; but even their mind and conscience is defiled.

Titus 2:

1But speak thou the things which become sound doctrine: 7In all things shewing thyself a pattern of good works: in doctrine shewing uncorruptness, gravity, sincerity, 8Sound speech, that cannot be condemned; that he that is of the contrary part may be ashamed, having no evil thing to say of you. 15These things speak and exhort and rebuke with all authority. Let no man despise thee.

Titus 3:

1Put them in mind to be subject to principalities and powers, to obey magistrates, to be ready to every good work, 2**To speak evil of no man,** to be no brawlers, but gentle, shewing all meekness unto all men. 9But avoid foolish questions and genealogies and contentions and strivings about the law; for they are unprofitable and vain.

Hebrews 4:

12For the word of God is quick and powerful and sharper than any two edged sword, piercing even to the dividing asunder of soul and spirit and of the joints and marrow and is a discerner of the thoughts and intents of the heart. 16Let us therefore come boldly unto the throne of grace, that we may obtain mercy and find grace to help in time of need.

Hebrews 11:

[3]Through faith we understand that the worlds were framed by the word of God, so that things which are seen were not made of things which do appear.

Hebrews 12:

[25]See that ye refuse not him that speaketh. For if they escaped not who refused him that spake on earth, much more shall not we escape, if we turn away from him that speaketh from heaven: [26]Whose voice then shook the earth: but now he hath promised, saying, Yet once more I shake not the earth only, but also heaven. [27]And this word, Yet once more, signifieth the removing of those things that are shaken, as of things that are made, that those things which cannot be shaken may remain. [28]Wherefore we receiving a kingdom which cannot be moved, let us have grace, whereby we may serve God acceptably with reverence and godly fear: [29]For our God is a consuming fire.

Hebrews 13:

[5]Let your conversation be without covetousness; and be content with such things as ye have: for he hath said, I will never leave thee, nor forsake thee. [6]So that we may boldly say, The Lord is my helper and I will not fear what man shall do unto me. [15]By him therefore let us offer the sacrifice of praise to God continually, that is, the fruit of our lips giving thanks to his name.

James 1:

[5]If any of you lack wisdom, let him ask of God, that giveth to all men liberally and upbraideth not; and it shall be given him. [6]But let him ask in faith, nothing wavering.. [22]But be ye doers of the word and not hearers only, deceiving your own selves. [23]For if any be a hearer of the word and not a doer, he is like unto a man beholding his natural face in a glass: [24]For he beholdeth himself and goeth his way and straightway forgetteth what manner of man he was. [25]But whoso looketh into the perfect law of liberty and continueth therein, he being not a forgetful hearer, but a doer of the work, this man shall be blessed in his deed. [26]If any man among you seem to be religious and bridleth not his tongue, but deceiveth his own heart, this man's religion is vain.

James 3:

[1]My brethren, be not many masters, knowing that we shall receive the greater condemnation. [2]For in many things we offend all. If any man offend not in word, the same is a perfect man and able also to bridle the whole body. [3]Behold, we put bits in the horses' mouths, that they may obey us; and we turn about their whole body. [4]Behold also the ships, which though they be so great and are driven of fierce winds, yet are they turned about with a very small helm, whithersoever the governor listeth. [5]Even so the tongue is a little member and boasteth great things. Behold, how great a matter a little fire kindleth! [6]And the tongue is a fire, a world of iniquity: so is the tongue among our members, that it defileth the whole body and setteth on fire the course of nature; and it is set on fire of hell. [7]For every kind of beasts and of birds and of serpents and of things in the sea, is tamed and

hath been tamed of mankind: 8But the tongue can no man tame; it is an unruly evil, full of deadly poison. 9Therewith bless we God, even the Father; and therewith curse we men, which are made after the similitude of God. 10Out of the same mouth proceedeth blessing and cursing. My brethren, these things ought not so to be. 11Doth a fountain send forth at the same place sweet water and bitter? 12Can the fig tree, my brethren, bear olive berries? either a vine, figs? so can no fountain both yield salt water and fresh. 13Who is a wise man and endued with knowledge among you? let him shew out of a good conversation his works with meekness of wisdom. 14But if ye have bitter envying and strife in your hearts, glory not and lie not against the truth. 15This wisdom descendeth not from above, but is earthly, sensual, devilish. 16For where envying and strife is, there is confusion and every evil work. 17But the wisdom that is from above is first pure, then peaceable, gentle and easy to be intreated, full of mercy and good fruits, without partiality and without hypocrisy. 18And the fruit of righteousness is sown in peace of them that make peace.

James 4:

11Speak not evil one of another, brethren. He that speaketh evil of his brother and judgeth his brother, speaketh evil of the law and judgeth the law: but if thou judge the law, thou art not a doer of the law, but a judge.

James 5:

9Murmur not one against another, brethren, lest ye be condemned: behold, the judge standeth before the door.

15And the prayer of faith shall save the sick and the Lord shall raise him up; and if he have committed sins, they shall be forgiven him. 16Confess your faults one to another and pray one for another, that ye may be healed. The effectual fervent prayer of a righteous man availeth much.

1 Peter 1:

23Being born again, not of corruptible seed, but of incorruptible, by the word of God, which liveth and abideth for ever. 25But the word of the Lord endureth for ever. And this is the word which by the gospel is preached unto you.

1 Peter 2:

1Wherefore laying aside all malice and all guile and hypocrisies and envies, all evil speakings, 2As newborn babes, desire the sincere milk of the word, that ye may grow thereby:

1 Peter 4:

11If any man speak, let him speak as the oracles of God; if any man minister, let him do it as of the ability which God giveth: that God in all things may be glorified through Jesus Christ, to whom be praise and dominion for ever and ever. Amen.

1 John 2:

5But whoso keepeth his word, in him verily is the love of God perfected: hereby know we that we are in him.

1 John 5:

7For there are three that bear record in heaven, the Father, the Word and the Holy Ghost: and these three are one.

Revelation 1:

[8]I AM Alpha and Omega, the beginning and the ending, saith the Lord,
which is and which was and which
is to come, the Almighty. [18]I AM he
that liveth and was dead; and,
behold, I AM alive for evermore,
Amen; and have the keys of hell and
of death.

Revelation 22:

[13]I AM Alpha and Omega, the
beginning and the end, the first and
the last. [16]I Jesus have sent mine
angel to testify unto you these things
in the churches. I AM the root and
the offspring of David and the bright
and morning star. [17]And the Spirit
and the bride say, Come. And let him
that heareth say, Come. And let him
that is athirst come. And whosoever
will, let him take the water of life
freely. [18]For I testify unto every man
that heareth the words of the
prophecy of this book, If any man
shall add unto these things, God
shall add unto him the plagues that
are written in this book: [19]And if any
man shall take away from the words
of the book of this prophecy, God
shall take away his part out of the
book of life and out of the holy city
and from the things which are written in this book. [20]He which testifieth
these things saith, Surely I come
quickly. Amen. Even so, come, Lord
Jesus.

[21]The grace of our Lord Jesus Christ
be with you all. Amen.

APPENDIX 5

Continued Study with
Robert Tennyson Stevens / Mastery Systems

DVDS - HOME STUDY COURSES

- Living the Path of Conscious Language™ 3 DVD set
- The Power of Imagination Activation 3 DVD set
- Conscious Prosperity 2 DVD set
- My Divine Partner Now 2 DVD set
- Sacred Body Language Translations 12 DVDs + BLT Book on CD
- Outcome Mapping DVD 1 DVD set
- All 6 DVD Sets (23 DVDs) Combined

CDS - HOME STUDY COURSES

- Upgrade Your Life CD
- Introduction to Conscious Language™ CD
- Conscious Language™ 101 3-CD set + mini-workbook.
- Imagination Activation Levels 1 & 2 4 CDs.
- Knowing & Attaining Your Dreams Now 2 CD's
- Conscious Prosperity 4 CD's
- Body Language Translations 1 CD
- My Divine Partner Now 1 CD.
- Mastery 201 Introduction 1 CD.
- All 20 CDs Set Combined

CD + DVD COMBINED SETS

- CD + DVD combo 1 Conscious Language™ 4 CDs & 3 DVDs
- CD + DVD combo 2 Imagination Activation 6 CDs & 3 DVDs
- CD + DVD combo 3 Conscious Prosperity 4 CDs & 2 DVDs
- CD + DVD combo 4 My Divine Partner Now 1 CD & 2 DVDs

BOOKS

- Body Language Translations Workbook Revised 2006
- Conscious Language!

ROBERT TENNYSON STEVENS / MASTERY SYSTEMS' EVENT CURRICULUM:

- Living the Path of Conscious Language™ 102 (1 day)
- The Power of Imagination Activation™ 102 (1 day)
- Sacred Body Language Translations WEEKEND™ 201 (2 1/2 days)
- MASTERY™: Embodying Conscious Language 201 (3 days)
- Mastery of Facilitation 301 (4 days)
- Mastery of Energies and Body Language™ 401 (6 days)
- Mastery of Commitment™ 301 (2 days)
- Body Electronics Level 1 and 2 (10 Days)
- Language of Mastery™ Instructor Training 401 (6 days)
- Outcome Facilitation™ Certification Training 501 (4 days)
- Bio-Optic Holography™ 201-601(weekend to 12 days)
- Language of Mastery by Certified Trainers.

For More Information: www.masterysystems.com

HOME STUDY AND EVENT DESCRIPTIONS

DVDS - HOME STUDY COURSES

Living the Path of Conscious Language 3 DVD set.
Conscious Language™ is the primary upgrade platform of Mastery Systems. This live, studio recorded Event takes the viewer though the Conscious Language™ Upgrade step by step. Each person planning to attend any workshop with Robert is requested to have this platform of understanding fully experienced before attending. You will be able to revisit this DVD Set many times to garner greater depth of understanding and apply the material with greater and greater results. Consider this DVD Set step one in the series.

The Power of Imagination Activation 3 DVD set.
Once the Consciousness Student develops the power of Conscious Language™ and Conscious Choice, the next step is changing the state of Consciousness from "being without" to "already having." The tools and techniques of Mastery Systems / Robert Tennyson Stevens provide immediate

results for the individual and the organization in shifting language and reality from limitation to abundance, aloneness to togetherness, conflict to resolution. This particular DVD Set is considered the second step for those studying at home.

Sacred Body Language Translations 12 DVDs + Body Language Translations Book on CD.
In the evolution of consciousness, our bodies are the storing banks of genetic, experiential, and collective (global) memories. Robert demonstrates the "other conversation" going on between individuals and within individuals through physical symbols, archetypal patterns, body sensations and energies in our environment. As new choices are engaged and lived, our body's language will confirm or deny our alignment with our new choices and language patterns. Consider this set of DVDs your premier self-alignment tool. Anyone committed to conscious communication, success, health, wealth, successful sales, effective coaching and clear facilitation will receive high quality, specific body language translations to enrich your ability to communicate and understand yourself and those you are supporting.

Conscious Prosperity 2 DVD set.
As Conscious Choice is engaged with Conscious Language™ and Imagination Activation successfully implemented, the viewer will have the opportunity to discover their Heart's Desires are possible and attainable. Prosperity is a Divine State, not just available for a chosen few. Understanding how to acquire what we desire and require is the responsibility of each Consciousness Student. Being Supplied is the only Truth to manifest. This DVD Set is for those ho have understood who they really are, and what they are really here for, and are committed to preparing the soil of their abundant garden, knowing what fruits they are passionate about harvesting, and lovingly and faithfully tend their soil until Divine Supply is realized.

My Divine Partner Now 2 DVD set.
Your twin flame, your Divine compliment already exists - looking for them is missing the mark. We have always been one with our twin love. Being our own Divine Partner attracts our counterpart. Merging with our creator is the first step to realizing our Oneness. This DVD Set will help the viewer behave as though they are already with their twin love and experience their own Divine Miracle in Consciousness until their Inner Reality becomes your outer Love! May this information bless you and remind you of your Oneness, your own personal brilliance, and your ability to be magnetic and draw your heart's twin to you now! First, be your own Divine Partner.

Outcome Mapping DVD 1 DVD set.
The more specific we are the more instantaneous the manifestation. Outcome Mapping is a form of Mind Mapping using Conscious Language™ and Outcome Facilitation which greatly enhance specificity and manifestation. The viewer will have the experience of increased Conscious ability to: identify current reality,

discover the vision, be clear on what actions to take, explore ideas into outcomes, and plan any strategy with greater success.

All 6 DVD Sets Combined All 6 DVD sets with 23 DVD's combined in one box set at special price.
Living the Path of Conscious Language o The Power of Imagination Activation o Conscious Prosperity o My Divine Partner Now o Sacred Body Language Translations o Outcome Mapping DVD.

CDs - HOME STUDY COURSES

Upgrade Your Life CD Single CD.
This is a new digitally mastered introduction to Conscious Language™, Imagination Activation, and Sacred Body Language Translations. A powerful primer to the Mastery Event or the Home Study Course. Great to start your understanding and introduce others to Mastery Systems' concepts.

Introduction to Conscious Language CD Single CD.
Step one in remembering the principles of speaking consciously. Our new digitally mastered introduction to Robert Tennyson Stevens and Conscious Language™.

Conscious Language™ 101 3-CD set + mini-workbook.
This is our core reality shifter. Words we use shape our thoughts and experiences just as a computer operating system instructs a computer. The feelings and emotions our words carry form our human operating system, which determines our reality. Just as one change in a line of software code changes an entire program; our alteration of even one word can change our entire experience of a specific situation. This CD Set is wonderful for reviewing the Domains of Self-Sabotage and their upgrades into the Domains of Self-Success.

Imagination Activation Levels 1 & 2 4 CDs.
Essential for each person committed to transforming life situations into highest choices. Far beyond simply rearranging the "known" options, you will learn to truly ACTIVATE your heart's most precious desires (often new to you). Including: How to get present, Current reality's power, The magic of outcome, Moving from A to B and then beyond, Identifying your action steps from your imagined outcomes, Activating imagination with vividness…

Knowing & Attaining Your Dreams Now 2 CD's.
Edited from RTSCC (Robert Tennyson Stevens' Conference Calls).Consider these two CD's introduction to and expanders of the Imagination Activation 1&2 CD Set. The RTS Conference Calls are a platform for Robert to share very focused concepts with the listeners in a short time segment. The material in this audio CD set uplifts, clarifies, inspires and initiates imagination with each listening.

Conscious Prosperity 4 CD's.
Edited from RTSCC. In these recorded conference calls, Robert addresses and reviews direct action steps to ensure the listener is aligned with Spirit and living in his or her abundant life. Receiving through others from Universal Supply instead of from others, Tithing, The Acorn Effect, Imaging From Already Being Abundant, and much more are covered in these four. A "must" if you have been experiencing lack of any good thing including money. The only truth is God is Abundance. Each CD is jammed packed with Robert giving steps and tools for success.

Sacred Body Language Translations 1 CD.
Edited from RTSCC. Discover how our bodies are literal interpretations of our subconscious minds and how to translate and upgrade any condition! Some live translations are given on this call.

My Divine Partner Now 1 CD.
Edited from RTSCC. Looking for your Divine partner is already missing the mark. We have always been one with our Twin Love. Being our own Divine partner attracts our counterpart. Merging with our Creator is the first step to realizing our Oneness. Act as if you're already with your Twin Love and experience your own Divine miracle unfold!

Mastery 201 Introduction 1 CD.
Here some highlights from live Mastery events hand picked by Robert to introduce the powerful principles of Mastery the Event.

Home Study Collection
Entire 20 CD set combined in one box set at special price: • Upgrade Your Life • Introduction to Conscious Language • Conscious Language 101 (3 CDs + mini-workbook) • Transforming Emotion Into Motion 101 (3 CDs + mini-workbook) • Conscious Prosperity (4 CDs) • Imagination Activation Levels 1 & 2 (4 CDs) • Knowing & Attaining Your Dreams Now (2 CDs) • My Divine Partner Now! • Introduction To Body Language Translations

CD + DVD COMBINED SETS

CD + DVD combo 1 Conscious Language Conscious Language 101 CD set + Living The Path of Conscious Language DVD set combined. 4 CDs & 3 DVDs.

CD + DVD combo 2 Imagination Activation Imagination Activation Levels 1 & 2 CD set + Knowing & Attaining Your Dreams Now Cd set + The Power Of Imagination Activation DVD set all in one album. 6 CDs & 3 DVDs.

CD + DVD combo 3 conscious prosperity Conscious Prosperity CD set + Conscious Prosperity DVD set combined. 4 CDs & 2 DVDs.

CD + DVD combo 4 My Divine Partner Now My Divine Partner Now CD + My Divine Partner Now DVDs combined. 1 CD & 2 DVDs.

OTHER BOOKS BY ROBERT TENNYSON STEVENS

Sacred Body Language Translations Book Revised

In the evolution of consciousness, our bodies are the storing banks of genetic, experiential, and collective (global) memories. In Body Language Translations, Robert visually describes how to "read" and translate how the subconscious communicates to us through symbols, archetypal patterns, body sensations and energies in our environment. Learning to "read" these patterns opens a whole new world of communication between our conscious mind and our "other than conscious" self. "Listen" to the language of the sub-conscious as it speaks through our hands, feet, face, eyes, nose, body movements, fingernails, hair, wrinkles, lines, symptoms, organs, glands, bodily functions revealing a dramatically deeper understanding of who we are, what our current requirements are and how best to respond with love. Please note, this is a workbook used in the Sacred Body Language Translation Courses and DVD Series. An electronic version is included in the Sacred Body Language DVD Series.

MASTERY SYSTEMS / ROBERT TENNYSON STEVENS EVENT CURRICULUM:

Living the Path of Conscious Language™ 102 (1 day)
The Power of Imagination Activation™ 102 (1 day) Usually given in a weekend called "Path and Power"

This multi-faceted weekend shows you how Living the Path of Conscious Language 102 creates success in your life -- at home, work and play. You also discover The Power of Imagination Activation 102 in receiving your highest choices in any situation. Imagine approaching every challenge and opportunity with your perfect outcome in focus. You CAN, and knowing how will change your life! This highly engaging introductory 2 day seminar includes interactive presentations, pod activities, personal writing and demonstrations on:

Sacred Body Language Translations WEEKEND™ 201 (2 1/2 days)

Sacred Body Language Translations 201 Weekend shows you the "other conversation" occurring within you, as your subconscious speaks through your body. You will also discover the amazing Grace going on all the time to help us, heal us, support us, love us and clear our way by some Inner Power, always active and functioning for our Great Good.

Our bodies store our genetic, experiential and universal memories and reveal a dramatically deeper understanding of where we are in consciousness, what we really desire and how to have our highest choice. Y ou will see a world of constant subconscious conversation taking place within our bodies through our: Hands, Hair, Eyes, Organs, Feet, Wrinkles, Nose, Glands, Face, Symptoms, Bodily functions, Body movements. Learning to "hear" and interpret our body language patterns opens a whole new world of communication between our conscious mind and our "other than conscious" self. Tools offered at this event are highly effective for anyone committed to personal and professional success in relationships as well as optimum health, love, facilitation and/or coaching.

Participants describe this material as among the most fascinating information they have received. Your tuition includes Mastery Systems' proprietary workbook. As with all Mastery Systems events, SBLT is conducted in a fun, interactive and emotionally safe environment.

MASTERY™: Embodying Conscious Language 201 (3 days)
This Event is our core upgrade experience designed to give the experience of embodying (feeling) new choices and new language patterns from the Heart. Highly experiential and transformative, those interested in being involved in Mastery Systems' Curriculum start here.

Mastery of Facilitation 301 (4 days)
With Mastery Systems' highly effective methods of self-facilitation, you learn to see your golden opportunities in situations you previously perceived as challenges. In Mastery of Facilitation (MOF), discover what has held you from your highest choices in the past, and how to apply your new Mastery Tools and Conscious Language™ in any life situation to achieve your heart's desire. Identify limiting thought forms as they happen, and transform them into your successful choices. Mastery 201 is pre-requisite.

Sacred Body Language Translation 401 (6 days)
This course is the Level Two for the Sacred Body Language Translations Weekend or DVD Set. Mastery 201 and Mastery of Facilitation 301 are also pre-requisites. Our body language is vast in revealing our inner truth and requires advanced Consciousness to understand its full conversation.

Mastery of Commitment™ 301 (2 days)
This course instructs us how to understand the dynamics of our "other-than-conscious-commitments" and discern the "conscious creative commitments" they have been suppressing. For anyone engaged in supporting others with life benefiting changes, MOC is a powerful investment for helping you recognize the "muck" is full of strengths waiting to happen. You will find this event is foundational for living your Conscious Creative Commitments.

Language of Mastery™ Instructor Training 401 (6 days)
LOMIT is a seminar, which addresses the technical aspects of Conscious Language™ with far greater detail than we do in our 3-day seminar. Designed as a Trainer Training, LOMIT 401 is for the perfecting of the intimate process of bringing Conscious Language™ to our Communities and Families. The LOMIT Graduate will, upon successful interview with Robert, be qualified to present Language of Mastery, a one or more day event to the Instructor's Community. LOMIT carefully reviews and amplifies self-sabotage and empowering language. Each Instructor is required to sign an agreement with Mastery Systems Corp. entitling you to teach LOM with your circle of influence. Each trainer sets their own fee and agrees to pay Mastery Systems a percentage of tuition moneys received. Many Trainers offer their events to schools, businesses, organizations, friends and family. Prerequisites: Mastery 201 & Mastery of Facilitation 301

Outcome Facilitation™ Certification Training 501 (4 days)
OFCT is excellent for self-coaching and for those who will be using Outcome Facilitation in success coaching settings. You will learn advance skills in breath, languaging, imagination activation and facilitation. The approach naturally reveals the strategies for being personally fulfilled in your own "big picture" (and coaching others to discover their strategies of personal fulfillment). The processes used in this event are extremely powerful, fast and remarkably simple. Superb for self-coaching and essential for facilitation practices dedicated to expeditious results. The Outcome Facilitation Certification Training helps you coach people to propel themselves into their ecstatic resolve and fulfillment. Trained in OFCT, instructors' skills are enhanced and they are able to offer personal sessions to their students.A special focus is placed on the exact questions which will ellicit a healing, upscaling response. The system Robert has developed has been shared with health practitioners, corporate executives, governmental officials, and Spiritually focused individuals.

Bio-Optic Holography™ 201-601(weekend to 12 days)
Studying your own eyes, and the eyes of others, offers a superb and intimate form of facilitation, personally and professionally. Bio-Optic Holography® is a series of tools to share with your family and loved ones. Each set of eyes displays your life lessons and "why you are here", as well as current reactions and responses to our ever changing environment. By examining the fiber structures, topography and layers of color in the iris of the eye, the vascular activity in the sclera, and facilitating with Conscious Language® and Outcome Facilitation®, a trained individual can easily resolve, understand, forgive and transmute long standing genetic and experiential reactions and limitations into choice and action.

For information:

www.masterysystems.com
Mastery Systems
(828) 891-7500
E-Mail: support@masterysystems.com

NOTES:

NOTES:

NOTES:

NOTES:

NOTES:

NOTES:

NOTES:

NOTES: